THE
FLORENTINE *Press*

RDR BOOKS

D0701705

Italian, It's All Greek to Me

RDR Books
1487 Glen Avenue
Muskegon, MI 49441
phone: 510-595-0595
fax: 510-228-0300
www.rdrbooks.com
email: read@rdrbooks.com
and
The Florentine Press
www.theflorentine.net
email: press@theflorentine.net

ISBN: 978-1-57143-171-4

Library of Congress Control Number: 2007930523

Distributed in the United Kingdom by
Roundhouse Publishing Ltd.
Millstone, Limers Lane, Northam, North Devon
EX39 2RG, United Kingdom

Distributed in Canada by
Scholarly Book Services
127 Portland Street, 3rd Floor
Toronto, Ontario, Canada M5V 2N4

Printed in the United States of America

Linda Falcone

Italian, It's All Greek To Me

**Everything You Don't Know
About Italian Language and Culture**

Illustrations by **Leo Cardini**

To my parents,
Robert and Lucia Falcone,
for giving me two countries

MENTALITY

TEMPERMENT

IDENTITY

Prologue

When my mother and father met, neither spoke the other's language. Although it proved to be a source of minor inconvenience, both chose to see language as a bridge rather than a barrier. Their real question was just how to cross the ocean between Italian and English. In the end the answer was easy: "Una parola alla volta," my mother said, "One word at a time."

Words are the stepping stones that lead you toward another world, and as part of a bilingual family, I've had more than enough words with which to build my bridges. Each language has had its purpose in my life and has often served me with varying levels of obedience. Although English is my native language, I find Italian more apropos for things like deep discussion, playful debate, and spontaneous prayer. I prefer English for both poetry and prose, subtle wit and brutal honesty.

Life in Italy has confirmed for me that every language is a product of its people and a faithful mirror that inevitably reflects a country's collective psyche. This series of vignettes is a celebration of Italian life and its labyrinths. Each expression discussed is meant to serve as a tiny window into the Italian identity. This book was written for those who know Italian and for those who would like to; for those who have visited Italy and for those who plan to; and also for those who've come here to stay for good, to live out their lives alternating cultural appreciation and culture shock. Culture shock, I'm sure, is one of life's greatest adventures. It is about acceptance, negotiation and transformation—three values indispensable to Italian living, because in this country you never know what stories the day will bring.

MENTALITY

Even the Eye Wants Its Part

Anche l'occhio vuole la sua parte

Italians relate food and beauty because they love both equally.

For three years I had the good fortune of living with two Italian painters. This is relevant to me mostly because when it was my turn to make a meal I always got painter-related commentary. They never told me how good or bad my food tasted. Instead, they'd say things like, "If you'd added a little green to this dish, it would have been *più bello*, more beautiful."

In Italy, nice people are said to be as good as bread. But good food in Italy can't be just good, it must also be beautiful. If I started to get huffy or whiny about my roommates' comments and protested, "What does color have to do with it?" they would shake their heads and say in wise voices, "*Anche l'occhio vuole la sua parte*. The eye also wants its part. To be truly enjoyed, food must also be beautiful."

"Beautiful" is not normally a word used in English to describe food, unless one is talking about the ice sculptures at a country club buffet or the roasted pork with pineapple served at a Hawaiian luau. English speakers might use "beautiful" to describe a seven-layer wedding cake, or a seven-dish traditional Japanese meal with lacquered chopsticks and edible flowers. Most would certainly not use the word "beautiful" to describe the unpleasant-looking brown rice and mushroom dish that Italians often refer to as *un bel risotto di funghi*. An English speaker would not ask for a beautiful dish of *prosciutto*, or a beautiful dish of *pastasciutta*. *Pastasciutta*, literally "dried pasta," is the expression that differentiates pasta like *spaghetti, tagliatelle*, and *farfalle* with sauce from *pasta in brodo*, or pasta in broth. Pasta in broth is also beautiful, by the way, and you will often be able to detect the underlying excitement in the voice of whoever sings the virtues of *un bel brodino caldo* on a winter evening.

I started cooking in Italy as a *principiante*, or absolute beginner. I quickly learned that by Italian tastes, my sauce was too raw and my pasta too cooked. To say the least, I had to start cooking from square one. When you are in square *numero uno*, you learn a few things. First, you are taught that salt and oil are good for you. Salt helps keep your blood pressure up, which is a positive thing, especially when the summer is humid and airless. Olive oil, on the other hand, serves to make your insides sufficiently slippery to ensure proper functioning of the kidneys. When cooking for Italians, one must consider food combinations and their effects on the bowel, texture, flavor, and especially color combinations and presentation on the plate.

When it comes to creating beautiful meals, colorful food is essential. Crowding your food is also unforgivable because, as before, *anche l'occhio vuole la sua parte*. Indeed, during one traditional meal in Italy each person uses more dishes than an American college student uses in a month. Once, when my grandmother was busy laying out seven plates per person, I told her in my candid "New World" way that it really wasn't necessary to change (and wash) so many dishes. She gave me a pained look and told me about the war. "When there was nothing to eat, we always had *una tavola nobile*, a noble table, with many dishes anyway," she said. It was no use trying to convince her. That was, of course, before I understood that crowding food is a sin. And no matter what I say to dissuade her, the table will continue to be noble even if the war ended fifty years ago and there is now enough food to feed an army.

Italians cannot help their craving for aesthetics. They easily relate food and beauty because they love both equally. Food is necessary for sustaining the physical body, and beauty is necessary for sustaining the soul. Thus, the combination of both elements provides pure nourishment. Italy, after all, is a country of artists. It is said that Italy is home to sixty percent of the world's art. Around here, food is another form of art. If you invite someone over for a meal, the food you serve has to have all the qualities of a good dinner guest. The menu should have flair, and it should be beautiful, creative, and independent. In order to truly satisfy, it should look like it's enjoying itself on the plate, because, after all, the eye does want its part.

The Shame of It All

La vergogna

The undisputed mistress of Italian society is guilt's fraternal twin: *vergogna*, shame.

It was *martedì grasso*, Fat Tuesday, and there we sat, thinking of how good we would have to be over the next forty days. My Aunt Donata had made *frittelle*— deep-fried fritters with pine nuts and candied fruit, made possible after two weeks of nagging. It's tradition for the old people to bribe the young people to save their orange peels. Donata makes them once a year and then invites her twenty nieces and nephews to crowd around her kitchen table and eat seventeen fritters each. Inevitably, when the last one is left in the bowl, someone will say *"Chi vuole quella della vergogna,* Who wants the shameful one?"

Now if you're new to this country, you might think that in this context the word *vergogna* comes from gorging yourself on eighteen fritters at an estimated fat content of twenty-six grams apiece. But you would be mistaken. Italians do not associate food with math, and know nothing of calorie counting. *La vergogna* doesn't come from eating the fritter, it comes from having to reach for the fritter. It's not committing the crime that's the issue, it's getting caught red-handed that really irks the Italian psyche. "Turn off the lights," Donata joked, "so nobody will see who's being greedy." Note that the key word there is not "greed," it's "see." It doesn't matter who eats *frittella* number eighteen; what counts is who's seen eating it. Now, this detail may seem insignificant, relevant only to the linguistically inclined. Trivial as it might appear, I'm convinced that this tiny nuance is a major clue to life in Italy. Learn the secrets of shame and many mysteries of *l'italianità*, Italian identity, will suddenly become as clear as the summer sky.

"There are two types of cultures in the world," my university professor Gustavo Forscarini told me one fateful day, "shame cultures and guilt cultures. Latin, Asian, and Arab societies are shame cultures; Anglo-Saxon, Germanic, and Scandinavian countries are guilt cultures."

"I grew up in a monastery near Palermo," he continued, "and I never wanted to kneel in church, ashamed as I was of the holes in my shoes." He laughed, "Had I been brought up in a guilt culture, I wouldn't have been so ashamed of my poverty. I would have been much more concerned about who was to blame for it."

Alas, unbeknownst to my dear Sicilian professor, I have been obsessing about his statement ever since. After ten years of collecting evidence everywhere, I've decided that I consider him perfectly right.

Upon observation, it's safe to conclude that in a guilt culture, if you trip on a crack in the sidewalk, spill hot coffee on your lap, or slip on a freshly mopped floor, it all comes down to who's to blame. That is to say, may the guilty party please rise so that we may shoot him down and take all his money. It's the lawsuit craze easily explained. I've discovered that guilt culture citizens are prone to feeling guilty about such things as spreading mayonnaise on their bread or taking a second helping of anything except celery. They torture themselves about trivial matters like not achieving their full potential, forgetting a birthday, or thinking about taking out the garbage but not actually doing it. Guilt is pervasive in a society where closed doors and perfectionism run rampant. Guilt, you might say, is a private phenomenon that a person suffers in the solitude of one's own mind-labyrinth. As natural strangers to solitude, Italians are seldom slaves to guilt.

The undisputed mistress of Italian society is, in fact, guilt's fraternal twin: *vergogna*, shame. And perhaps if guilt is a private obsession, then shame is a collective affectation. Ever-present queen of the piazza, shame is common in Italy and other cultures where family obligation and community pressure make saving face the primary goal of all citizens, both young and old.

"Italians feel shame because everyone is always looking. The bread lady, the neighbor, the neighbor's dog, *tutti*. Even Donata pulls her summer laundry in at midnight to see who's coming home with whom and at what hour," my cousin Giovanna teased our host, as she reached for *la frittella della vergogna*.

"Listen," I told my crowding audience, "In the U.S. a student sued a donut shop for twenty thousand dollars because he slipped on a freshly mopped floor. He won because the court ruled that there should have been a sign saying 'Watch your step; WET FLOOR.'"

"What's a donut?" my cousins wanted to know.

"Sort of like a *frittella* with a hole in the middle."

There was hearty laughter everywhere.

"The fritter man cleaned his shop and had to pay twenty thousand dollars!" Giovanna paused a moment, chewing thoughtfully. "Better shame than guilt," she mused. "Shame is much cheaper."

Blasts of Air

Un colpo d'aria

You might be unaware that
air is a dangerous element.

Homeopathic doctors will tell you that illness starts at a psychological level and has to do with your state of mind. Not only that, it also has to do with the state you happen to be living in. Life on the Italian peninsula has convinced me that health, in reality, is a cultural variable. Try, for example, to be sick in Italy. Just for the sake of cultural research, complain that you have a pounding headache. Say that your eyes are redder than usual or that you have lacerating stomach pains. The closest you will get to sympathy is the ever-present Italian expression used to dismiss every minor medical calamity: *"Si vede che hai preso un colpo d'aria.* It seems you have been hit by a blast of air."

If you haven't been living in Italy long, you might be unaware that air is a dangerous element. Hurricanes and tornadoes aside, you may be under the impression that a little bit of good air can do a body no harm. Think soft spring breezes. Think wind rippling through amber waves of grain. Think open car windows on a summer drive through the country. Now forget about it. Italians will have none of it. According to popular belief, *un colpo d'aria* is the number one bearer of bad health in Italy and should be avoided at all costs. Mention a dull ache at the back of your neck or a sudden pain in your lower abdomen, and the culprit will always be found in the end. Usually air takes the blame as *causa causorum* of anything from sore gums to strep throat.

Last June, I was driving with a group of friends through the countryside in Emilia Romagna. We were driving alongside a field of poppies toward the sun, but we could just as easily have been on it. There we were, windows rolled up, five of us melting in the old Fiat Punto that my friend Alessandro had been able to borrow from his sister, having promised to clean the upholstery afterward. Needless to say, the air conditioning didn't come on that day. "I'm boiling! Can we open the windows?" I yelled, trying to be heard over the Genovese lawyer singing cabaret music on the radio.

"Do you want us all to wake up with a sore neck tomorrow morning? We can't open the windows now. We'd all get *un colpo d'aria* for sure," Alessandro answered, incredulous.

If he was incredulous, I was beside myself. "Ale, it's 45 degrees Celsius outside. We would be *lucky* to get hit by some air!"

My friends laughed, but still the windows didn't budge. No one would risk it. "Getting hit by air when you are sweaty is the worst thing that can happen. It's very bad for you," Alessandro explained.

"Is it as bad," I asked, "as getting hit over the head with a pogo stick?" Nobody knew what a pogo stick was, but it wouldn't have convinced them anyway.

In winter, of course, it's worse. During my first Florentine winter, I came down with the flu. As expected, most people blamed my influenza on *un colpo d'aria. Signora* Ida, our third-floor neighbor across the alley, went a step further. Having seen no undershirts on my clothesline, she had known I would catch something sooner or later. Didn't I know that going out in winter without a *maglietta della salute*, a health shirt, was a risk? Of course, the fact that the neighbor lady was talking freely about my underclothes shocked no one but me.

Invariably, if you get sick in Italy you are sure to learn many things. Be sick in this country and you will discover the secrets of wellness. Black licorice is good for your blood pressure. Honey heals all ailments. If you put a raw potato in your mouth it will heal your toothache. Wire bracelets combat rheumatism. Artichokes are good for your liver. Lemons treat colds and flu. Sulfur springs are good for asthma. Garlic is for bronchial problems. Boiled bay leaves and lemon rinds work on stomach pains. Blueberries are good for your eyes. And, most importantly, an undershirt can save your life because *aria* is a risk, especially if you're imprudent enough to get blasted by it.

Into the Wolf's Mouth

In bocca al lupo

It is extremely bad luck to wish someone
good luck in the literal way.

In Italy it is good luck to touch iron. Knocking on wood will do nothing for you. It is also good luck to touch the hump of a hunchback or stroke the nose of a wild boar. Fortune will also smile kindly upon you if you jump when you see a priest or play 47 on the lottery wheel after you dream of a dead relative. I am told that rain on your wedding day is really good, too.

It also may be useful to know that in Italy it is considered extremely bad luck to wish someone good luck in the literal way by saying *buona fortuna*. The lucky way to wish good fortune is to say *in bocca al lupo*, which can be translated as "into the wolf's mouth." Similar in tone to the English expression "break a leg," the *in bocca al lupo* metaphor compares any challenge to being caught between the hungry jaws of a wild beast whose aim is to swallow both the unfortunate and the careless. The "wolf" may be a teacher who wants to fail you or a critical audience before a presentation at work, or it could simply symbolize having to overcome any excruciatingly difficult enterprise. (And yes, buying a stamp and a lightbulb in the same morning can be classified as an excruciatingly difficult enterprise in Italy.) I've learned a lot of lucky things in my Italian life, but sometimes bad luck comes along when it shouldn't.

My first year at the *Università degli Studi di Venezia*, I stood in line for an oral exam on medieval history. Things appeared to be going considerably well. We were only half an hour past the scheduled exam time and, according to reliable sources, the professor was actually somewhere on the premises.

Where exactly, nobody knew. There were roughly a dozen of us waiting for him in silence, as if we were third-graders in line for confession trying to think of what to say to the priest. The sentiment was actually quite apropos, because our classroom was part of a de-consecrated church now used for city council meetings and higher education. Dr. Di Cataldo lectured from where the altar used to be, and judging by my classmates' expressions, at least half the class wished the hall were still a place of prayer. On this particular day, a girl I had seen wearing a fur coat several times that term smiled and offered me a toffee, so naturally, I forgave her for her cruelty to animals. We started to chat.

"It's supposed to be a really tough exam," she said, "So, *in bocca al lupo.*"

"*Grazie*," I smiled.

In response, the fur-coat girl gave me a pained look and took a step back. Thanking someone for wishing you good luck is the surest way to earn yourself really bad luck. The appropriate response to *in bocca al lupo* is *crepi*, or "may the wolf die." But what if you are distracted and worried about getting toffee off your teeth before your turn? What if you forget to issue the death threat?

"*Ora ti sei messa in un vero pasticcio!* You've gotten yourself into a real *pasticcio* now!" another of my classmates whispered.

As you might know, *pasticcio* is a giant lasagna that women traditionally make with fresh pasta for Sunday dinner. It is also a synonym for serious trouble or a big mess. Admittedly, there are occasions when getting trapped in a delicious giant lasagna doesn't sound like such a punishment. This was not one of those times. The thought of *pasticcio* did not appeal to my queasy stomach, especially if I was supposedly swimming in it.

By the time the professor arrived, I was a nervous wreck. *Studente numero uno* stepped apprehensively into the examination room and emerged fifteen minutes later looking as if he had just been to the dentist. I was *studente numero due.* With resignation, I sat across from Prof. Di Cataldo and awaited my fate. "Speak to me of the major forces that influenced medieval literature," he said.

I spoke of superstition, powerlessness, and questions of free will. I explained the concept of man's destiny being dictated by unknown forces and the whims of Fate and Fortune. When I got to the part about man's struggle for knowledge against all odds, I started to get emotional. Fortunately for me and history, that undercurrent gave birth to the Renaissance Man.

When I left the testing room and emerged victorious from the beast's belly, I wasn't wearing lasagna. I was wearing a big smile. You might say I was one lucky Little Red Riding Hood. My exam had gone well. And the wolf? That bad old *lupo* was good and dead.

It Depends

Dipende

Ask an Italian to take a stand on what you consider a clear-cut issue and what you'll get is a good case of juggling.

In the middle of a lesson, my student pulls her desk up closer so we can understand each other better. In Italy, it's best if you can touch whomever you're talking to. Before traipsing into my classroom three weeks ago, Marilena had never studied English. Her generation speaks French. She decided to pay for individual lessons so that we can produce only conversations that interest her personally. She's too old to be bored with nonsense, she says. Supposedly it's one of the benefits of being fifty-five.

As of yet, our conversations would not entertain a fly. There's only so much you can do with the verb "to be" and a handful of adjectives. "What is your favorite color?" I ask in my slow-mo voice.

Marilena thinks a moment and answers me in Italian 'Color? *Dipende.* For what? A room? A jacket? For eyes? Cream for a room. Black for a jacket. Green for a man's eyes.'

"No, I just mean, your favorite color, in general."

"But that's impossible to say. *Dipende.* It depends if I'm in love or feeling angry. It depends if the color is for curtains or for flowers."

Hmm. It ends up she likes blue when she's in love. Orange when she's angry. White is her favorite if we are discussing drapes. Yellow is her choice color for flowers. Except roses. Red is best for roses. Unless they are growing on a bush. Roses should be pink when in gardens.

I know I should have stopped her at her first word in Italian. After all, she is paying me to force her to use her thirty-word English vocabulary. I should have snapped my fingers and said in my mean governess voice, "English only please." But I couldn't. I was more than impressed with my student's ability to delve so deeply into the world of chromatic preference. Also, I am fascinated by the Italian dependence on the word *dipende*. For years, their incessant use of the word has filled me with wonder. In Italy, no simple question has a simple answer. Most things must be qualified, and virtually everything depends. Ask an Italian to take a stand on what you consider a clear-cut issue and what you'll get is a good case of juggling.

After school, I met my friend Francesca for hot chocolate. Classes with Marilena, sweet as she is, always leave me in need of liquid energy.

"It was a stupid question, really," Francesca argued, when I complained about my student's inability to commit to a color. "She's right that each shade has a special role in our lives."

"Fine," I sighed. "It's a superficial question. But, I couldn't very well ask the woman to discuss existential theories. She knows four words. And anyway, that's not the point. Is it that Italians are unable to give straight answers or do you just avoid them on purpose?" I asked.

"Both, I suppose." Francesca smiled, "We say *dipende* because we are too creative a people to be tied to one possibility only. But, *dipende*. It could also be out of fear of what others will say. With several responses, there is a better chance of saying something acceptable."

"So you're afraid someone will use your favorite color against you?"

"The politicians always do."

"Luckily, I'm not a politician."

"Yes, but I am. And most Italians are."

"What is that supposed to mean?"

"That we look for advantageous situations and then search for allies."

I rolled my eyes and my friend explained. In Italy, opinion caters to convenience. What could, should or must happen depends more on circumstance than on personal conviction. What is pleasurable today may be painful tomorrow. A friend today may be a foe tomorrow. In both world wars, for example, Italian diplomats switched sides when the going got rough. In 1945 it took them two weeks to tell the troops that the Germans had become enemy soldiers. Italians have learned the hard way never to commit too strongly to any one idea. It's best to keep one's options open. In this country, one never knows when the tides will change, and they always do. Italy has four seas to prove it.

"Italians have non-negotiable loyalty to football clubs and their mothers. Everything else depends." Francesca concluded with a grin.

I looked at my friend and frowned. I just didn't have the strength to consider the implications of that statement. What did it mean to live in a society where mothers and soccer teams merit the same level of loyalty?

But, at least one thing was certain. I should have ordered whipped-cream with my hot chocolate. I might have found some comfort in it. Why is it that as soon as I find the answer to a pressing cultural issue, another question pops up to disturb my new-found sense of order? No sooner is one mystery solved than another begins. That is how it is to live in Italy. It's a nice country, but it offers no rest for the weary.

It Simply Isn't Done

Non si fa

Non si fa experiences are crouching in corners all over Italy like accidents waiting to happen.

Italians, as a people, are fairly relaxed. They will not obsess about politically correct word choice or nitpick about pseudo-moral dilemmas. They have a great capacity for putting things in perspective and avoiding unnecessary fuss. But there are some things that you cannot do in Italy. Some things that are just not done. Have never been done. Will never be done. Why? Simply because *non si fa*. *Non si fa e basta*. They are not done and that is all. No explanation offered, no justification provided. In this country, *non si fa* is reason enough.

I've started keeping a *non si fa* list and often ask for contributions from those of us who, through trial and error, are slowly discovering the taboos of Italian society. So here are just a few of my favorite things that are just not done in Italy. No walking barefoot ever or anywhere. Plastic beach thongs are often worn to avoid touching shower tiles in hotel bathrooms, and slippers are used for in-house lounging. No showering after meals. It blocks the digestion and could be deadly. No shorts in the city even if it's August. This is especially true for women. Skirts are much more attractive. No eating without a tablecloth. Even Italian college students have an aversion to bare tables. They're not beautiful. At the very least, you can opt for placemats (which, incidentally, are known as *tavolette americane*). No using toilet paper to blow your nose. Cloth hankies are common even for men. No carnations or chrysanthemums unless you are on your way to the cemetery. No parmesan cheese on fish pasta. No mixing sweet and savory. No washing your hair every day. Even the hairdresser will say that it's unhealthy, and that oil is a good thing for the scalp. No breezy open windows, even if there is no draft within a 30 kilometer radius. No cappuccino after a meal. And please, no itemizing the bill. Get over yourself. If you go out with the same friends with some regularity it will all even out in the end.

Non si fa. Non si fa. Non si fa. These may seem like minor Italian idiosyncrasies that can simply be overlooked by the magnanimous and liberal-minded. Maybe, but the truth is, Italians are not free-thinkers. They are fun, creative, and sometimes brilliant, but they are not free-thinkers. Social expectations occupy too much of their psyche. Moral obligation and tradition have dibs on at least eighty percent of their personal choices. So if you plan on staying in Italy long, you'll soon discover that the *non si fa* admonition is a big fat hairy deal, especially when it comes to intercultural relationships and day-to-day survival.

Take my friend Jonnel, for example. She married her Italian husband two years ago in Florence. Believe me when I say that Jonnel is not the obsessive wedding-planner type who felt compelled to micromanage her special day. She wanted a simple do-it-yourself type of wedding where the guests actually had a good time. She also wanted centerpieces to decorate each table, and, since it was a winter wedding, she thought to opt for simple bouquets of brightly colored tulips. The florist would not oblige. "*Non si fa,*" he said. "You cannot have tulips for weddings in Italy." The fact that she wanted to get married with tulips and was willing to pay for them made no difference. Why? Tulips are not a wedding flower. Period. Jonnel was left both tulip-less and speechless. Such formal anti-flower convictions are hard to swallow for someone who comes from a place where you can get married in a drive-thru wedding chapel.

Alas, *non si fa* experiences are crouching in corners all over Italy like accidents waiting to happen. Go to the good sandwich place on *via dei Neri*, and scout out the selection of delicacies that can go between two slices of salty *foccaccia*. "I'd like a *panino* with *prosciutto cotto*, *stracchino* cheese, and creamed artichoke hearts," you tell the guy behind the counter.

"No. I can't give you that combination."

"Why not?"

"*Non si fa*. Two soft ingredients will turn to mush."

Don't do it. Don't insist. Don't tell him that you like mushy. Don't tell him that you've been craving mushy all day. It doesn't matter. Just let him give you the sandwich he thinks you should eat. In Italy, once *non si fa* is out of the bag, there is no way to win. *Non si fa. Non si fa e basta.*

Let's Get to the Point

Arriviamo al punto

Italian easily lends itself to circular thought.

E nglish speakers follow a straight line; Italians talk in circles. If you engage in intercultural communication on a daily basis, this is something you probably already know but possibly have never thought about. So let's think about it now, shall we?

I'll start by saying that Italians are generally recognized as entertaining speakers. Their enthusiasm is contagious, and their conviction is constant. And yet, as my friend Phyllis says, "Sometimes you can listen to an Italian involved in dynamic discourse and find yourself wondering just where they are going with it. *'Arriviamo al punto,'* you want to say in your diplomatic English-speaking way, 'Let's just get to the point!'"

Hah! Easier said than done, my friend, easier said than done. Try to make an Italian obediently *arrivare al punto* and you will come to the same conclusion I've reached after years of struggle. You'll discover that there are two types of speakers in the world: linear speakers and circular speakers. Linear speakers look for the shortest distance from point A to point B. What do I want to express and what is the shortest way to get there? Clarity. Precision. Well-clipped elegance. That's what the Linears want in a language. And English lends itself to this expectation quite nicely. In English, every sentence comes out the same way, as in subject first, then verb, and finally object. Speaking English is like linking wooden blocks that always have to be laid out in the same order.

Italians, on the other hand, can leave off the subject or choose to start from either side of the sentence. Affirmations become questions just by the lilt of the voice. In Italian, there are at least four ways to say something just by modifying word order. In short, Italian easily lends itself to circular thought.

If you don't believe me, think about how English speakers tend to organize their thoughts. Have you ever met an English speaker who could not produce an outline on demand? It's all about A, B, C, and 1, 2, 3. A topic sentence and three main ideas. No delicious digression, no tempting tangents. None of the redundancy and freedom abundant in the Latin languages.

Italians have many talents, but most cannot produce an outline when asked. In Italy, knowledge is a wheel, a series of spokes radiating from a central nucleus. You start from the main point and take one of a thousand radii. Therefore, in Italian, digressions are not true digressions, and tangents are considered an integral part of what English speakers would call "the point."

So next time you are caught in a whirlwind of Italian verbosity and find yourself hoping in vain that your *amico* will *arrivare al punto*, there's something you need to remember: Italians have been educated in a school system that favors interdisciplinary thought. It's a philosophy born in the Renaissance, during which the goal of education was to cultivate genius. Leonardo was an artist, scientist, and engineer. Michelangelo was a sculptor, painter, and architect. Lorenzo dei Medici was a politician, patron, and poet. To an Italian that still means something.

The circular model of knowledge still profoundly influences Italian education today. At the end of each term, teachers get together in a meeting called *gli scrutini*, which comes from the root word "scrutinize." Giving grades is a negotiation process that looks a bit like bartering. The math teacher has a say over the English grade. The science professor has to approve the score awarded in art history. To the linear-minded, it may seem unfair, but according to the Italian perspective, it is completely logical. After all, can art be divorced from science? To succeed in grammar, you need to have a basis in mathematical principles. To excel in the figurative arts, a knowledge of anatomy is essential. This means that the grading process translates into, "If you lower the math grade, I'll raise the student's grade in history." The goal is to arrive at a well-rounded score that allows the student to achieve a passing mark in every subject.

So, when your favorite Italian speaker has lost you entirely and has gone off on something you perceive as completely unrelated to her original *punto*, remember that in Italy, seemingly unrelated topics are very relevant to each other. So, just relax and let her lead you through the labyrinth. You're better off not resisting it. And although it's true that the shortest way from A to B is a straight line, while living in Italy never underestimate the power of the circle.

Politics Are a Dirty Thing

La politica è una cosa sporca

Never let their faux optimism fool you.

S itting on a terrace in Chianti, happy as a clam, I was enjoying my first meal *al fresco* in eight months. It was my friend Edoardo's birthday and the spring air was crisp and the company warm. Then suddenly the winds changed.

"So, the government has fallen at last," Edoardo announced between slices of pear and *parmigiano*. He said it with as much indifference as an Italian can muster, and it was received with as much apathy as his dinner guests could feign.

"Finally!" his wife mused, without looking away from the fruit cups she was serving.

"They gave you a good birthday gift, *amico mio*," our friend Ruggero joked. "This year you don't have to wish Berlusconi away with your birthday candles. It seems like he will be going away by himself!"

There was laughter everywhere.

Italians face political turnover with unnerving nonchalance. Most are convinced that taxes and bureaucracy will stand strong whether the government falls, rolls over, plays dead, or gets back up when no one is looking to pour itself a cup of coffee. I, of course, was the only one who was concerned.

I come from a country where governments don't just fall between the second and third course of a meal. And although I could appreciate the unfailing Italian ability to good-naturedly adapt to new situations, I found my friends' reaction a bit worrisome. Like it or not, hadn't Berlusconi been elected by the people? In a respectable democracy shouldn't the prime minister be able to fulfill the five-year term guaranteed him by the constitution? What would the failure of his government mean to Italian politics? What would it mean to me as a citizen?

While I silently wrestled with democratic principles and the modern world, the topic of conversation moved to soccer. *Mamma mia*! Being served our first strawberries of the season had kept the group's attention for longer than the governmental crisis. And there was no doubt that *la Fiorentina*'s match against *Juventus* the night before was weighing more on people's minds. Apparently the "violet" team's loss was more essential to the Florentine sense of well-being than the loss of a prime minister. And as pleasant as dinner *al fresco* was, I found the prospect a bit infuriating.

Edoardo's wife, Silvia, who is good at reading people's minds, saw something in my expression that invited her to explain. "Over the past fifty years, we've had forty governments and no change. It's like choosing the kind of gelato you want, except all the flavors taste the same. When *il Parlamento* feels the prime minister's not doing an acceptable job, they give him a *voto di mancanza di fiducia*, lack of faith vote, which often means he's forced to step down. It's a loophole in the system created to protect Italy from another Mussolini. It's built into our system. Most times, they just piece things back together, like in that rhyme of the egg that had a great fall."

"But doesn't it matter to you?" I asked. "If the government fell like that in the U.S., citizens would suddenly feel very vulnerable and lost. Half the population would end up having to go to Tahiti to find themselves."

"Well," Silvia laughed, "then they are likely to find our

politicians there. Several fled to tropical islands after the *Tangentopoli* corruption scandals in 1992. Those were hard times for Italy. Many politicians ended their careers that year, either in jail or by suicide. Quite a few left the country and became beach bums. But most of the real bums are still running the country. In Italy, *la politica è una cosa sporca.* Politics is a dirty thing."

Silvia's statement got the rest of the group talking government again, mostly because Italians never miss an opportunity to express their inborn cynicism. Yes, that's right, cynicism. Never let their faux optimism fool you. Despite the happy-go-lucky image they often project to the world, deep down Italians are, invariably, fatalists. It might not seem so at first glance, but in the end, for Italians, it is about the inevitability of death and taxes.

After most of the guests had gone, my host slung a lazy arm around my shoulders, "Still thinking *politica*?"

I nodded. "Sorry to beat a dead horse, but I just don't understand what will happen now that the government has fallen."

Edoardo stifled a smile. "Unfortunately, nothing. But if it worries you, have faith. Berlusconi will be back again tomorrow."

And indeed he was. It took a little over a week and then all the king's horses and all the king's men properly patched poor Humpty Dumpty together again.

We Can't Do Anything Until September

Non si fa niente fino a settembre

In August, holiday trips are the only things that can get done with any level of reliability.

When living in Italy it may prove useful to synchronize your watch. It's also indispensable to coordinate your calendar. The first step is to be bold and rip out the month of *agosto*. Nothing worthy of putting on a calendar can be done then anyway. In Italy, August is a strange month, during which a city like Florence has people pushing at it from all sides. Half the people are eagerly aiming to get in and the other half are hell-bent on getting out. The incoming crowds are mostly made up of travelers and artists visiting the city as part of their *"Italia: città d'arte"* tour. The outbound crowds include the majority of its natives, who interpret *agosto* as the word for mass exodus.

In *agosto* all the people worthy of putting on your calendar, such as doctors, dentists, house painters, and accountants, have either gone to the beach or are busy congregating in the mountains. If you're a tourist, or someone stranded in the city working for groups of them, be aware that goods and services are often in high demand and low supply during the month of August. After all, it's a vacation month, and holiday trips are the only things that can get done with any level of reliability. Most people, however, can remember vacation departure dates without the help of little numbered squares.

It's the time when Italian city businesses are rigorously *chiuso per ferie*, closed for holiday, and even those poor straggling employees left to hold down the desolate fort will most likely refuse to get any sizeable jobs done. If you do find a professional handyman around, he'll most likely dismiss the urgency of your faulty plumbing by saying, "*Non si fa niente fino a settembre,* nothing is to be done until September."

And now that you're familiar with the phrase, allow me to properly warn you: *Non si fa niente fino a settembre* is more than just the off-handed musings of an unwilling handyman who's eager to get himself off the hook. We're talking about the summer excuse *par excellence,* and it's in the mouth of everyone. Let's just say that in Italy it's simply culturally inappropriate to expect your needs to be addressed before the beginning of September. No other justification is necessary. August is excuse enough.

Why? Because it's common knowledge that in the face of *ferie,* holidays, your household emergencies become entirely irrelevant. It doesn't matter if you find yourself stuck with a month of no hot running water. Cold showers, they'll tell you, are good for circulation. They improve blood flow. No matter how embittered it makes you feel, remember, the blood they're referring to is yours.

Now in defense of the *non si fa niente fino a settembre* phenomenon, the heat of summer in Italian cities does not allow for high levels of productivity. In a valley city like Florence, where air is scarce and humidity high, even fulfilling basic necessities like eating and sleeping require unusual effort. It's understandable that all one really wants to do in the heat is take care of one's plummeting blood pressure by sucking on lemon and licorice. I'd also recommend strawberry and coffee gelato, tall glasses of water with mint, generous portions of buffalo mozzarella, and thick watermelon slices (though not together, please).

On really desperate days, pay a visit to the Watermelon

Man, whose stand graces *Piazza dell'Indipendenza*. For two euro, he'll set you up with the fattest watermelon slice in Florence. Evenings there with good friends and great fruit are among the best advantages of the Florentine summer. As far as I can see, the Watermelon Man has two things going for him. He'll never sell you a bad slice, and he'll never ask you to get moving. At most, he'll tell you to bring your own chairs next time you come.

But the day will suddenly arrive when his watermelons are not as crisp as before. And that's the sign. Call your plumber. *Settembre* is coming around the corner soon enough and you'll want to be first in line.

It's Not Part of Our Mentality

Non fa parte della nostra mentalità

Some of us get to the point where Jell-O becomes
the source of a high-profile crisis.

If you've just arrived in Italy and are kicking for a little *avventura italiana*, you're probably still feeling excited and optimistic. Most likely you're convinced that if you ever decided to stay long term, you'd never get homesick enough to miss something as trivial as Jell-O. Maybe you won't. But some of us are not that strong. Some of us get to the point where Jell-O becomes the source of a high-profile cultural crisis.

If you know people outside of Italy who love you, one of them might get the brilliant idea of sending you imported treats like Pop Rocks and Fruit Roll-ups. If someone does, be careful with whom you share them. Things like that don't exist in Italy. Italians love food, but they simply don't like to play with it. *Non fa parte della nostra mentalità*, it's not part of our mentality. My first year in Italy, a friend sent me lime Jell-O, which at the time was the equivalent of green gold. Eager to share my edible treasure, I invited my cousin Leonardo to experience one of the true joys of American cuisine.

When he is not busy infuriating me, Leo is one of my favorite people in the world. My summer partner-in-crime growing up, he was my first and best Italian culture teacher. He was privy to all sorts of scary Italian knowledge that all children should be safely versed in. For instance, leaving an uneaten grain of rice on your plate will keep you out of paradise; rotting pomegranates in your fruit bowl will earn you wealth one day; and the smell of stinky feet can blind you. As far as I could see, Leo deserved a taste of American culture for a change.

It is not often that one gets to act like a mad scientist, unveiling a discovery that could revolutionize European culture in one's lifetime, but that is how I felt as I pulled the top off my Jell-O container. "You'll love it!" I told my cousin as I set out the cups, barely able to contain my excitement.

Leo, however, didn't share my enthusiasm. "Sorry," he said, shaking his head, "but we don't eat green slime food in Italy. *Non fa parte della nostra mentalità.* It's not part of our mentality."

I stared. "You mean you'll eat donkey stew, goat brains, and cow kidneys but you will not eat lime-flavored gelatin?"

"I just don't share your passion for edible rainbows," he smiled wryly. "Don't take offense."

I should have known. Because they boast the world's best cuisine, Italians have no reason to be adventurous eaters. Most prefer to avoid the unknown at all costs. Still, I glared at my cousin, incredulous. Leo was snubbing my Jell-O. If there were ever a reason for harboring silent lifelong resentment, this was it. "I'm not offended," I said, slamming down the serving spoon. The Jell-O trembled a bit in its bowl. I was not going to cry, though. Crying over dessert is definitely wimpy.

"Don't be so *americana* and tell me you are not offended when you are," he said.

"Don't you tell me what to be!"

My cousin is often an idiot, but he was smart enough to know that he had somehow really hurt my feelings. He tried again. "It's nothing personal, Linda. But why eat something that probably cannot be considered food? *Non fa parte della nostra mentalità,*" he repeated. "It's just not part of our mentality."

"Jell-O is not part of the mentality?"

"No."

"*Who cares about your mentality*! Lots of things around here are not part of *la mia mentalità*. I do them anyway. It's called being adventurous! It's called being open-minded. It's called being polite!"

"It's called food poisoning!" my cousin grinned. Leo would not give up. He had spent all his life in a culture where he could joke his way out of anything. Apparently, he had never used his Italian charm on Jell-O before.

Then something unexpected happened. I don't know what made him do it, but perhaps he knew he was really in trouble. Leo stacked his fork and knife onto his abandoned plate and brought it into the kitchen. Angry or not, I was witnessing a miracle. I don't think he had ever cleared the table in his own house before. As an Italian son, taking his dish to the sink was also not *parte della sua mentalità*.

Then my cousin stuck his head out of the kitchen doorway, looking sheepish and loveable even if I didn't like him at all. He raised his eyebrows and then winked. "Come on, lovely, let's eat that *Jell-O* before it melts. Let's eat it in front of the TV so I can be a true *americano*."

"*Impossibile*."

"Come on! I will tell you it's good. I promise."

"Too late, Leo."

"You *americani* show no mercy. That is why you have capital punishment."

I looked at my cousin. "Why do you have to make everything into a cultural issue? Can't it just be about two people eating dessert, no matter what country they're from? I think if you prepare a dessert and your friends refuse to eat it, they're being rude no matter what country they're in."

"In Japan, men who eat desserts are considered softies."

"Do you have to know everything? Can't we just have a simple conversation with no cultural trivia in it?"

Leo was having a hard time. He looked down and decided he was going to have to play it my way. "I'm sorry I hurt your feelings about your dessert." He said it very quietly and his apology made me want to forgive him. It would be enough, I decided, if he would just understand one simple thing. "There's something you should know about Jell-O, Leonardo. And that is—Jell-O is important to me."

"Alright," he said. "Should we eat it then?"

"I'm still kind of mad."

"Alright, we should eat it then," he said, piling a wobbly spoonful into his mouth. "It's good," he told me.

"We made Jell-O brains in the fifth grade," I said, my enthusiasm suddenly returning.

Leo couldn't see why one would eat Jell-O, but he could definitely conceive making a science experiment out of it. "Do you think that if I threw this at your head it would bounce back?"

Reaching high levels of cultural understanding and mutual respect for cultures is quite a challenge. Maybe world leaders should eat Jell-O together, that's Leo's final analysis. It's true. How serious can you be about your own little issues when you are eating a food that bounces?

TEMPERMENT

Don't Take It Personally

Non te la prendere

What most English speakers call "being insulting"
Italians describe as "being sincere."

Years of Italian living have taught me that one must be brave when talking to Italians, mostly because they will always tell you what they know. If you have gained a kilo and someone notices, which is probable, they will tell you. If the hairdresser went overboard with your hair cut, you won't be left with any doubts as to what people really think about it. If you've been invited to dinner and have a pimple on your nose, be prepared to have your host tell you very frankly and in all politeness, "I see you have a pimple." In fact, not only will he remind you that you have it, but he'll also tell you how to get rid of it. A lengthy debate will ensue among guests, and everyone at the table will simultaneously suggest a different method to solve your unfortunate *problema dermatologico.* Some will recommend milk to soften your zit, others will suggest you spread toothpaste on it before sleeping to dry it out. (Personally, I prefer the toothpaste method).

Whether or not you find the *cura* you need, I've learned the hard way not to take personal offense when it comes to well-intentioned comments and criticism. It's best to listen to the friendly admonition—*non te la prendere*— which can mean anything from "don't take it personally," to "don't take it seriously," or "don't get worked-up over nothing." In fact, if you plan on staying in Italy for a long time it will prove an essential mantra for day-to-day survival. I'll even go further by suggesting that adopting the *non te la prendere* philosophy will help safeguard the health of all your intercultural personal relationships. This is true, in part, because what most English speakers call "being insulting," Italians define as *essere sincero*, being sincere. *La sincerità* is an art form in Italy, and creative insults are said to add both humor and color to any relationship.

Take, for example, the uncanny Italian talent for taking your worst fault and making it into your nickname. If you're short, they'll call you *Nano*, "Dwarf." If you're fat, they'll call you *Ciccio*, "Chubby." If your head is big, they'll call you "Melon" or "Pumpkin" or "Big Head." If your big brother has a big head, they'll call you "Little Big Head." If you have ears that stick out, they'll call you "Dumbo." Obviously, if your nose is long, you will be "Pinocchio." You can also be called Pinocchio if your legs are short because, in the original Italian version of the story, some liars had long noses and some had short legs. In my Venetian high school, I had friends who were sadly christened with all of the above. Except Pinocchio, of course. It's just too long. Our big-nosed friend was Pino, which rolls far more easily off the tongue.

As Italians see it, if you have short legs or a big head, and everyone knows your head is big, and you know your head is big, then why pretend that it isn't? "We just feel it's best to get things out in the open. We take our shortcomings and make them into good jokes," my cousin Leonardo told me recently. "In Italy, we offend for affection."

Well, happily, I have received my fair share of affection in the last fifteen years. I've been *Zingara* (Gypsy, for walking around the kitchen in bare feet), *Zanze* (after a crazy lady who used to live in San Frediano), *LuLu dei Fiori* (after a cartoon character whose nose turns up like mine), *Senzasangue* (for having cold hands in both winter and summer), *Fantasma Formaggino* (the cheese ghost, no idea why), and more recently, *Pinguino* (supposedly for the way I walk).

"But what if I don't like being told that I walk like a penguin?" I asked Leo, feeling very justified in my self-pity.

"Ahh, *Pingui, non te la prendere*," he replied. "Penguins aren't that bad, considering all the things we could tease you for."

Needless to say, I felt much better after that.

Nice People

Gente simpatica

If we can't change it, then at least
let it serve to entertain us.

It's Day Five of their study abroad adventure in Florence and my students are worried. Overseas for the charm of glossy exported Italian-ness, most are shocked to discover that the Italians they've encountered in the bars, banks, and Benettons throughout the city are as expressive as *baccalà*, dried salty codfish. Where, they wonder, are the jolly pizza-making Marios they expected? Where are the whimsical, wiry-haired Benignis? How come the friendly, happy-go-lucky Italians that populate their collective consciousness are not out roaming the piazzas?

"The people here aren't very nice," a student will invariably tell me.

"Well," I say with a knowing nod, "being nice isn't a Florentine goal. They don't see themselves as 'nice people.' They are *gente simpatica*, but not nice people."

"I thought *simpatico* was the word for nice," she protests. Yes, it's true. Most heavy dictionaries and harried language teachers will tell you that. It's a question of simplicity. In reality, though, the two words are actually quite different. *Simpatico* has a lot more to do with being smart and fun than it does with being nice. "Nice" describes those polite positive thinkers of indisputable moral fiber. *Simpatico* has none of the same do-gooder implications. Nice people remember to call you on your birthday. They send thank-you notes and are the first to RSVP to written invitations. *Gente simpatica* just show up and are the life of the party.

In English, nice people are out there to make a difference. *Gente simpatica* are not. Often slightly cynical and very comfortable with jest, *gente simpatica* are not aiming to make the world a better place. They are already quite satisfied with how things turn out. After all, *gente simpatica* know how to flip the *frittata* and make ugly things bearable by the sheer cleverness of their wit. "If we can't change it, then at least let it serve to entertain us," my colleague Niccolò tells me often. "Yes, the traffic is horrible, the politicians corrupt, and the wages ridiculous, but we can still decide what to laugh at." Indeed, *gente simpatica* serve up humor in all its scalding sincerity, and swallow it down equally well, without watery eyes. It's a Tuscan talent, you see, to tell it like it is.

For *gente simpatica* there is only one source of activism, and that is to tell the truth. It may sting a bit for those who hear it, like a bandage coming off a scab, but there's delicious freedom in it for everyone. Someone who's nice, on the other hand, tends to be a bit of a ninny. One has to be very careful not to offend the sensibilities of nice people. After all, kindergarten teachers are nice. The girl your mother wants you to marry is nice. Big Bird and Mr. Rogers were nice. Oscar the Grouch was not; he was selfish and had matted hair. But you liked him anyway, and maybe you even liked him best. Grouchy but *simpatico*, he could make you smile.

My students, lost on the possibility of Oscar the Grouch being of true Tuscan character, stare at me blankly. Granted, it could be because it's Monday and most have been on a train from Paris all night in a half-hearted attempt to get to their morning class on time. It could also be because I am full of hot air, and the difference between "nice" and *simpatico* interests no one but me and the Oxford Dictionary Man.

When I let the class go for our *pausa caffè*, I am happy to find Niccolò, my ultra-*simpatico*, left-wing colleague, already at the coffee machine. He may not be the Oxford Dictionary

Man, but frankly, he is the next best thing.

"Listen Nico, I had an idea in class today," I say.

"*Sentiamo*, let's hear."

"Do you know any Florentines you'd call 'nice?'" I ask.

"This is the most beautiful city in the world. You want nice, too?" he responds, grinning just in time to curb his arrogance.

"Yes," I tell him solemnly, "I want the beauty of Italy and sweet serviceable people who tell me to have a nice day."

"So go to Orlando, *bimba*," is my friend's reply.

Bimba, the word for "little girl," is an expression of Tuscan affection and, for me, it seals the deal. I'll take *simpatico* any day of the week. Except maybe on Sundays. My mother taught me that, if you can, it's always best to be "nice" on Sunday.

A Timid Population

Un popolo timido

We like to talk but don't necessarily
want people to listen.

If you really want to make an Italian squirm, politely listen to what he has to say. Sit with your hands in your lap and nod attentively after each of his emphatic affirmations. For an Italian, there is no worse scenario. Why? Because Italians are fundamentally shy. "*Siamo un popolo timido*, we are a timid people," my friend Luciana told me one day. "We like to talk but don't necessarily like it when people listen to us."

Certainly, Italians are not known to the world as a *popolo timido* for all the talking they do in piazzas and at parties. And granted, "shy" might sound like a strange way to classify this extremely social race that is happiest among people, *passeggiate*, and parades. And yet, I've found Luciana to be right in what she says.

But if neither of us can convince you, you'll just have to wait for autumn and find out for yourself.

Humor me. On the fourth Thursday in November invite twelve of your closest Italian *amici* to share roasted turkey and red berry jam. After you've convinced them that it's okay to alternate bites of fruit salad and mashed potatoes, try to get them to play what I call the Gratitude Game.

Halfway through the meal, inform your guests that it's a Thanksgiving tradition to go around the table and take turns saying what each guest is thankful for. If you are an American by birth, I'm sure you know the routine. One person talks and the rest of the group listens attentively as all the people seated around the table reveal their improvised pearls of wisdom.

It's that wonderful way of communicating that English speakers also know as the "what did you learn in school today" style of discourse. The host, or the head of the family, initiates conversation and the guests, or children, as the case may be, obediently indulge in alternating bouts of speech and quiet.

"I'll start," you say to your Thanksgiving crew. "I am thankful for good friends, cornbread muffins, the Boboli Gardens, and purple cyclamens." Odds are, your proclamation of gratitude will be followed by embarrassed silence. This is simply because Italians have not been trained to express themselves when everyone is listening. God forbid, they might get caught saying something stupid; for an Italian, that is a fate worse than death.

Admittedly, Italians have no problem boisterously expressing even the most controversial viewpoints in an impassioned effort to be heard over the twelve other equally adamant communicators populating your dinner table. All is well when one is surrounded by the safety of chatter. But give them a silent space in which to speak, and what you'll find is a *popolo timido*, just like Luciana says.

English speakers are different that way. Most will only speak if there is room. In an English-language environment, having to fight to be heard is considered, at best, chaotic and, at worst, uncivilized.

For an Italian, the exact opposite is true. Simultaneous discourse is the dynamic key to all illuminating expression, and not only that, it's a safe place to hide.

The point is, if you want to have a successful dinner party with members of this *popolo timido*, forget about circular games of gratitude. Give them a nice animated group of guests willing to talk to death about the superiority of Canadian apples. Let them glide in and out of the tap dance of simultaneous discourse and resign yourself to being the wallflower at a high school dance. I promise that your timid guests will go away grateful.

One Must Be Awake

Uno dev'essere sveglio

Make many friends and find out
what they know.

Amongst the innumerable laws that crowd the Italian constitution, I'm told there's one about pedestrians having the right of way. I, however, have never seen it happen in real life—and I've been keeping my eyes open.

In college, my friend Domenico and I were inseparable. He is originally from Puglia but was studying in Venice, so in a way, he was almost as foreign as I was. He just knew a lot more. Everything, in fact. But it's something I often overlooked because I knew he'd grown up with a father who quoted Latin poets during dinner and a mother who made him learn about Doric and Ionic columns on Saturday afternoon outings.

One morning, as we crossed *Campo Santa Margherita*, he said, "You're lucky we live in Venezia. In a real city you'd get run over with the way you walk in your sleep."

"What's that supposed to mean?" I frowned. Domenico was my best friend and very good at unnerving me.

"In Puglia, cars speed up rather than slow down when they see you waiting to cross. Really, you're not too good at paying attention. People from the New World always walk like you do, with half their brains turned off, as if the world were a field of daisies."

"What do you mean?" was all that came to me at the time.

"To live well in Italy, *uno dev'essere sveglio*, one has to be awake. Italy is a dangerous place for those who sleep. You have to keep your eyes open and look out for yourself."

Hmm. Twelve years have passed since he made his comment,

and I am still wondering what I should have said in response. Sometimes people just knock the wind out of you. Since then I've moved to a city with cars and learned that *sveglio*, awake, is the highest compliment an Italian can bestow. Why? Because despite all of their socialist policies, Italians root for the survival of the fittest. They are firm believers that success should come only to those who learn to stay awake.

Time in this country has taught me that, unlike citizens from more civic cultures, Italians don't believe in systems. In Italy, for example, policy is not seen as protection. The government is the enemy. Laws do not increase order. Signs are not to be trusted. Public service messages touch the heart of no one. Traffic laws and exact tax payments weigh lightly on the collective psyche. Bureaucracy is seen as an incurable Italian disease. If you must deal with the system, cunning is key. Domenico would often say, "If you can't beat them, join them. And if you can't join them, trick them. And to trick them, you've just got to be awake. If you are, then no one will take advantage of you."

If you're new to Italy and still walking in your field of daisies, all this may sound a bit like paranoia. That's what I thought. But then I said, "Fine. This is Italy. Let's play it your way. But, may I ask, just how does one go about becoming *sveglio*?"

Domenico liked my question. "It's simple," he smiled. "Make many friends and find out what they know. Knowledge is indispensable to survival."

It did not take long for Domenico to prove his point. By that time we had reached the courtyard of *Ca' Foscari*, the university building. By the way, if you plan on taking a trip there, don't go through the main door. It's against the law. It's also life threatening. The main door, which was built by Marco Polo's first cousin, is perennially under restoration. It will fall on your head if you go near it. In many countries a similar source of public peril would be blocked off, barricaded, and guarded by the National Guard. Here they don't even put up a warning sign.

Everybody just knows not to go that way. Luckily, "awake" Italian students are willing to let you in on cute info like that. But I thought I'd tell you as well, just in case you don't know any students or have no *sveglio* friends to tell you what thresholds not to cross. It's knowledge that could prove necessary. However, if you do have a Domenico of your very own, do what I do and let him cross under the alcoves first.

Italians Speak With Their Hands

"Gli italiani parlano con le mani"

In Italy, conversation is theater.

My cousin Carlotta is twenty-five and has been for the past five years. She was born six years after her brother and I but stayed younger only until she learned to talk. Those were the good old days. Carlotta is what Italians call *una peperina*. It means she has spunk and fills her words with red pepper. As of today, she is studying to be a tour guide. It's the right job for my cousin because she always knows exactly where she is and how she got there. She is no more beautiful than anyone else, but you notice her in a crowd. She looks like someone who knows where all the commotion is coming from and most of the time, it's coming from her.

For me, Carlotta is the epitome of Italian expression. Verdi's melodrama is in her genes. For Carlotta, speaking is not an action, it's a state of being. She enters into it. I watch her talk often. Arguably, most Italian speech is worth watching more than it is worth hearing, because in Italy, conversation is theater.

Italians are known throughout the world for being talkers. They talk across alleys and through open windows. They talk over tables and tiny cups of steaming black pitch. Italians talk in piazzas every night until eight o'clock, when the inaudible dinner bell rings and sends everyone back home to their respective tables. Italians talk about food, politics, love, and neighbors. Then they talk about children and mothers, pain, piety, food again, and then bodily functions. They talk in church, on trains, while standing at crosswalks and while waiting in butcher shops. To speak with smooth words and wide gestures is a favorite national pastime, and it should surprise no one to say that *gli italiani parlano con le mani*, Italians talk with their hands.

You've seen it, of course. How they lift their words with high, vibrant gestures meant for raising spirits or eyebrows, or how easily Italian hands find humor and squeeze it from the air as if they were wringing out a dripping sponge. Italians have hands that scold or feign indifference, encourage laughter, or diminish the distance between two minds. For an Italian there is nothing like a low scoffing wave to chase problems away. In this country, speaking without gestures is like writing without punctuation. Hands are commas, exclamation points, and question marks; words are lifeless without them.

We could attribute Italian gesticulation to the peninsula's artistic past. Roam the streets of Italy's *città d'arte* and it will all become clear to you. Italians are artists by nature, with hands destined to create by means of paint, wood, or marble. What other culture throughout the ages has been so able to give life to stone and gently coax the soul from the inanimate? In the absence of brush and chisel, the air itself becomes a means of expression.

The habit could also stem from the Latin flair for the theater. Italians are, after all, children of the Greeks. By right of birth and ethnic heritage, Italians are natural masters of tragicomedy, and their piazzas become a ready stage for a thousand personal theaters.

Carlotta invited me to dinner one night and refused to let me do anything. Thank God. Next to her, I am the definition of inept. She stood at the kitchen counter talking and cooking. I sat contentedly playing with silverware as she rolled out homemade *gnocchi* like a machine. Every two *gnocchi* or so she would stop rolling and dramatically sweep her hands through the air to emphasize the point she was making.

"Are you capable of talking without your hands?" I teased.

She put her flour-covered palms on her hips and answered, peppery as usual, "Why would I want to? To be like English speakers and lack conviction? They speak from their mouths only. Italians don't just talk with their hands, we talk with our whole bodies. We step into speech."

"You make speech sound like a dance," I said.

"Is it not?" she smiled, returning to her dumplings.

Well, there you have it. *Italiani*: the same hands they use to salt their foods, they use to salt their conversations.

To Have Liver

Avere fegato

To live well in Italy you need three things: cunning, luck, and liver.

I'd been recently hired by a Tuscan regional association whose goal was to provide youth services and career training to young Italians who wanted to become more desirable candidates for the international job market. During a workshop on writing resumes, my student Claudio, raised his hand to adamantly proclaim the uselessness of the lesson.

"This is a waste of time," he protested, "because none of us are going to get the job we want anyway. It's an impossible thing."

Unsure of how to react to his outburst, I tried to make light of his comment. "Well, you can always use a scrap of your resume to stop the table leg from wobbling," I told him.

He smiled and the lesson went on virtually undisturbed, but suddenly my heart wasn't in it. When the workshop finally ended, I went to talk to Domenico. When I am plagued by that feeling of futility that teachers are often known to experience, he is the person I most like to see. Not that he ever tries to make me see the bright side of things. Remember, Domenico is from Puglia where fatalism is a way of life. He listens patiently first, and then he proceeds to artfully wrap my worries in a thousand long-winded theories until I've forgotten my original dilemma. Our visits usually solve my chronic cultural distress quite nicely and I go away quite comforted. There is nothing as reassuring as someone telling you that you're being an idiot when you really are.

"Domenico," I complained, "these students in my class are twenty-six years old and most have never had a paying job before. Half of them are apprenticing in law offices or architectural firms for free. It's degrading. When I asked them what their professional goals were, most just went on and on about how difficult it is to work in Italy. They seemed so resigned and dreamless."

Domenico thought a minute and I waited. Whatever it is he wants to tell me, he usually takes the scenic route to get there. "Well," he said, "it used to be that to live well in Italy you needed just three things: *furbizia, fortuna, e fegato,* cunning, luck, and liver. Young Italians have the first two but are miserably lacking in the last."

"They lack liver?" I asked, not realizing that he meant to say they had no guts.

"Yes. Our generation was born with no courage at all. We are not risk takers because we have known too much comfort. Besides, we have no use for *fegato.* In Italy, there are no more new horizons. Everything has been done. That's why you used the word 'dreamless.' Every inch of creativity has already been claimed."

My friend's comment left me surprised and silent. "Is that true?" I wondered. Has Italy, home to more artists, saints, and adventurers than any other part of the world, suddenly become a sterile country? Modern architects certainly had a hard time, I knew. After all, new buildings easily become eyesores when crunched between the Roman and the Gothic. And it's well known that innovation is not a key word in many Italian cities, where people need official permission to paint their shutters any color other than olive green. New artists, I've also been told, find it hard to produce when the whole world is still feeding off the wonders of Michelangelo. And scientists? Did we know any graduates, Domenico demanded, who had been awarded research grants in Italy? No. All had been forced to find support abroad.

"In Italy the young have become pessimistic," Domenico continued. "Maybe in America people feel their pioneer past. There's still the idea that you can go west, put up a stake, and claim new land. Americans put up a flag and claimed the moon. In Italy, it's not that way. Here, everything has been discovered. And what hasn't been discovered is best left underground."

"What do you mean?" I asked.

"Try to build a house here. As soon as you start digging, you unearth Etruscan ruins. So you have to stop construction to preserve history."

I sighed. He had so many words and I so few. "You're not making me feel better," I said.

"Nor did I have that intention," my friend grinned. "You know, the difference between you and me is the way we look at a tree. You find all this depressing because Americans value far-reaching branches. Italians don't. We prefer far-reaching roots."

That's what I like about Domenico. He makes you wait an hour and a half, but in the end, he's always able to summarize cultural identity in twenty-five words or less. It's a talent, however, I can't afford to give him credit for. Act impressed by Domenico's axioms and it's the end of you. "You should have been a *filosofo*," I told him, with all the indifference I could feign.

"Of course," he grinned. "If you don't have *fegato*, you need *filosofia*."

There it was again. Life in a nutshell.

Prego

Prego

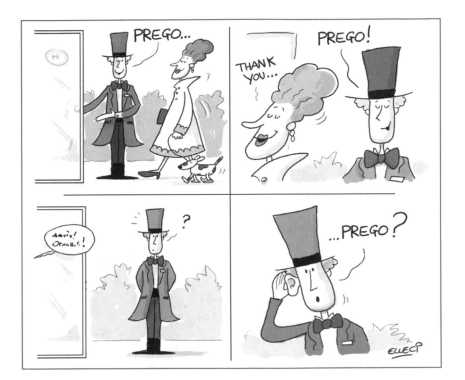

Prego is the multipurpose solution
to every linguistic need.

If the Italian language is a locked door that you're still struggling to open, then I've come to bring you the key. No matter how many subjunctive verbs your language teachers want to fill your brains with, all you really need to get by in this country is a whole lot of *prego*. There are some words in the world that carry their weight in gold. There are some words that travelers should keep safely jingling in their pockets at all times. Some words are like spare change that can be easily spent in tight times. *Prego* is one of those words. It opens all doors. And in Italy, you'll find it everywhere except ladled over your pasta. *Prego* is the multipurpose solution to your every linguistic need. Just what does it mean? Well, everything, actually.

Spend a week or two in Italy and you'll see. *Prego* implies serviceable attention, it commands respect, and it encourages people to either wake up or speak up. Bread-selling ladies in their crisp, candy-striped uniforms will shout it at you from behind mounds of soft *focaccia*. Harried postal workers will bark it at you from behind their Plexiglas protective shields. Newfound friends will shower you with *prego* as a sign of their dutiful affection.

When expressed as a question in shops and markets, *prego* means "Can I help you?" or "What can I do for you?" It's the invitation to ask for what you need. It's your chance to become that demanding client that Italian shop owners love so well. When expressed as an affirmation, *prego* grants permission. It means "Of course," or "Certainly," or "Be my guest." "May I come in?" *Prego.* "Do you mind if I open this window?" *Prego*. Thus, an initial exchange in a shop might sound something like this.

"*Prego?*"

"*Posso dare un'occhiata?* Can I have a look around?"

"*Prego!*"

In more informal situations, *prego* is often accompanied by props or gestures that modify its meaning. When accompanying wine and water or wooden plates of antipasti, *prego* means "help yourself." When uttered alongside an empty chair it becomes "please have a seat." Say *prego* to an older lady when you are in a line at the grocery store and you mean "feel free to go ahead of me since you are only buying milk." Say it after someone profusely thanks you and you will mean "you're welcome" or "cheers." Say it when someone's mumbling or speaking too fast and you will mean "I can't hear" or "I beg your pardon?" *Prego* can also imply elegant disbelief or subtle nonconformity, and it is a favorite power word for all age groups.

Add the object pronoun *ti* to *prego*, and you will drastically enhance your communication abilities. With *ti prego*, you'll find a plethora of essential idioms suddenly on the tip of your eager tongue. Put your hands in front of your chest in the praying position and you suddenly have "I beg of you" or "have mercy." Roll your eyes and toss your head and *ti prego* becomes "Give me a break, will you?" All very useful expressions, I might add, for those planning on staying in Italy for a long time.

So aren't you happy to have such a lightweight, no fuss, highly practical word to tote around the peninsula? For many frustrated English speakers learning Italian remains a quasi-mystical process, a journey through the dark forest of linguistic confusion. If you are one of them, a word like *prego* is like the sun shining through the trees. Or perhaps I'm being too dramatic. Perhaps the Italian habit of adding poetry to the most banal word stew has seeped into my cells. If so, *ti prego*, humor me. Because we really are talking about a magic word. It's not just "please." It also means "you're welcome" and almost everything in between.

Check, Please

Il conto, per favore

In Italy, we pay our waiters to disappear.

" *Il conto, per favore."* That's how you ask for the check in Italian. And now that you know, you might as well forget it. It's not worth your brain space. I mean, you can ask for the check in restaurants in Italy, but, most likely, no one will bring it to you. Why? Well, because around here, checks are brought at midnight. To receive one anytime before Cinderella's curfew is considered insulting because Italians go to a restaurant for the table space as well as for the food.

"Italian flats are small and space for meeting friends is limited. Going out to eat is like renting space to talk," my friend Marco explained. I smiled in response. We were sitting at a table in our favorite Florentine trattoria, and although it certainly has a lot to boast about, space is not one of its strong points. If it was space we were renting by dining out, we certainly weren't getting our money's worth. Most nights we were forced to sit with other diners at a table that was hardly suited for two in the first place.

But, no worries. Italy has taught me a lot about the art of inevitability. When dining in this country, certain things are inevitable. No matter the restaurant, you'll almost always find too many tables crowding the floor space, no *conto* until closing time, and waiters who don't give their customers the time of day.

Before you rush to defend your favorite waiter, let me explain. Italian waiters are highly qualified and very competent. Most will briskly bring your plates of fried zucchini flowers and *pecorino stagionato* with fig jam and not have to ask who ordered what. They can even do it without having to write down your order. They simply have a feel for what each person looks like they should be eating. Still, *camerieri* are often so abrupt and serious in their serving style that diners new to Italian eating are often left feeling more like a burden than like a paying customer.

I mentioned this idea to Marco, and he scoffed, "Waiters aren't here to be your friends. They're here to serve you quality food at the right temperature and in the right order."

"Fine," I argued, "but why do they have to make you feel like you're bothering them?"

"At least they don't sing like all the waiters in Los Angeles do. It's enough to make you lose your appetite. On my last trip, in every restaurant I went to, my meal was interrupted by waiters singing the happy birthday song at the top of their lungs. Do they have to be songbirds to get hired over there?"

"Well, no, waiters in L.A. aren't singers. They're actors."

"Ah," my friend nodded, "so that's why they all smile with thirty-two teeth and tell you their name. They're hoping to find an agent at one of their tables."

I laughed. "They try to be nice so people will leave a big tip."

Marco was unconvinced. "But what do I care what the waiter's name is?"

"You are a snob," I told him. It was an insult that he didn't find insulting in the least. In this city, there is prestige in snobbery, so I was forced to try a different tactic. "At least American waiters don't disappear from the face of the earth in the middle of your meal like Italian ones do."

Marco laughed. "In Italy, we pay our waiters to disappear.

We don't pay them to ask us annoying questions or tell us about their favorite opera stars. Everywhere I went in California, as soon as the waiters found out I was Italian, they would tell me how much they liked Pavarotti."

"You're exaggerating."

"No. I go out to eat for a little privacy. If I wanted someone breathing down my neck, I would have stayed at home."

"Part of the fun of eating out is to have the waiter talk to you," I argued.

"If I wanted to answer questions during dinner, I would have gone to my mother's. But why are you obsessing about our waiter? Do you want to have dinner with *him*?"

"No, but if you're feeling threatened and want to get rid of him, all you have to do is say, '*Il conto, per favore.*' He'll never come back again," I replied.

It was a memorable moment. For once, my friend had no comeback. For once, I had won a Florentine debate. And believe me, it is better than being treated to dinner.

It's Difficult

E' difficile

E' difficile is not actually a negative reaction.
Italians like difficult things.

D uring my university years, I had the great fortune of living right above a Venetian canal. The apartment's floor was uneven in places and its mosaics rippled as if someone were slowly pulling them from under your feet. There were high gothic windows and the sound of boats knocking together to rock me to sleep. It was perfect. The only sore spot was the spot of mold growing on the sitting room ceiling.

By December it had flourished into a furry modern art tapestry. Quaint, possibly, but I'm not particularly fond of sprout-your-own mildew wall-hangings. "Do you think you'll be able to paint the wall before Christmas?" I asked my boyfriend, Claudio, in my tenth request for whitewash.

"*E' difficile.* It's difficult." he told me. The wall would need to be isolated or it would just happen again. There would be dust and the smell of paint which would undoubtedly give the cat allergies. We'd have to break the wall and get permission from the neighbors—and maybe even the city. That mold might mean we'd have to restore the whole *palazzo*.

If you're a creative person full of bright ideas about how the world should work, be prepared to hear your share of *è difficile*. Not that eliminating mildew is that creative an idea, but it does stretch beyond the realm of standard daily routine and thus falls into the *è difficile* category.

My gut reaction was to scold, bribe, and argue that fungus away. Just in time, I remembered that *è difficile* is not actually a negative reaction. Italians like difficult things. It gives them a chance to show how smart they are. *E' difficile* is simply the Italian way of throwing the bait. Bite at the hook and you're a goner. Argue your point and all you'll get is ten more minutes of tirade.

You want to do that? Don't you realize how *difficile* that is? This is Italy. Things are hard here. There are laws in the civil code against this. We'll need a notary for sure. Whatever it is, it will cost too much. Whatever it is, we don't make enough. It is not done. It simply cannot be. This is not the New World, you know. We've fought wars here. We've been invaded. Italy is a conquered country. The Greeks, the Spanish, the Arabs, the French, the Austrians. We can't do that. *E' difficile.*

Yes, well, I've been hit with obscure historical references long enough to know that there is nothing Italians like more than a bit of history. It makes the word stew meatier. For an Italian, history justifies all modern-day behavior. If your boyfriend doesn't feel like painting the ceiling, his motives can be traced to the fact that the Visigoths conquered Venice during the Barbarian era.

Don't worry if you don't know who the Visigoths are. The point is, if justifications can be fished from the jaws of history, then solutions can be found there as well. You have to fight fire with fire. So if you know nothing about the Roman Empire, look it up. It's the key to unlocking all Italian potential. No matter how *difficile* an enterprise, mention *l'impero romano* and the winds will change. Having once ruled the western world makes for modern-day optimism. Used sparingly, Ancient Rome opens all difficult doors.

"Do you think you'll be able to paint the house by Christmas?"

"*E' difficile.*"

"You know, I'm always so impressed by the Romans' capacity

91

to build such amazing roads."

"By Christmas, you say? Hmm. I'll see if my brother will help me."

See? *E' difficile* is just a signpost on the road to somewhere. Don't let the barricades fool you. In this country, there's always a way through. So when you encounter the expression, nod and avoid argument. After all, the only way to win with Italians is to trick them. It's a very anti-English language principle, I know. But sometimes, difficult times and moldy walls call for desperate measures.

We'll See

Poi vediamo

Poi vediamo means "Let's have several plausible options
and be willing to abandon them without
the slightest raise of an eyebrow."

Just relax. Take a deep breath. Abandon Plan A. Leave it at the bus stop before you mount bus 14. It's already too crowded in there. Leave Plan A at the bottom of the stairs before you brave the five flights up to your room with a view. It's heavy and you'll have little use for it. On a good day in Italy, you'll need Plan B. Most days, though, you'll be forced to trade all plans for *poi vediamo*. One of Italy's most common expressions, "later, we'll see" keeps the door to adventure wide open.

Ask an Italian a clear-cut, future-based question. Do you want to go out to dinner? *Poi vediamo*. Are we going to Arezzo this weekend? *Poi vediamo*. Will you be able to pick up the dry cleaning? *Poi vediamo*. In Italy, it's never as simple as yes or no. Dinner may happen. Arezzo might be possible. That errand may get accomplished. It isn't safe to say just now. Later, the path will become clearer. After all, life does have its way of producing unexpected obstacles.

Don't get me wrong. Italians are not spur-of-the-moment people. They enjoy comfort too much. Most will not venture anywhere unless they know where they are going and what types of food they will find there. *Poi vediamo* does not mean "Let's do something spur-of-the-moment ." Nor is it an expression of optimism suggesting that life is bursting with endless possibility, as in "The world is wide and wonderful, so let's not tie ourselves down to a plan." Italians are far too fatalistic to suggest throwing caution to the wind and becoming free spirits.

The virtue of *poi vediamo* also does not lie in a genetic

aversion to planned events. Generally speaking, Italians have no problem with thinking about the future. Most will invite you to make as many plans as you please. Just don't be so foolish as to have faith in them. Around here, plans will most likely produce unintended results. That's the secret. *Poi vediam*means, "Let's have several plausible options and be willing to abandon them without the slightest raise of an eyebrow." After all, in the Italian world one never knows what detours await the lowly adventurer.

You plan on doing your laundry this morning? You're aiming to visit the bank? You want to scout out the market across town for shoes on sale? Certainly all worthy, if not ambitious goals. But have you considered the threat of a bus strike? Or what if the bank clerks have abandoned their desks in hopes of a raise? And laundry? What if the power goes out? What if you inadvertently use more than your legal share of household energy? Hair dryer, radio, and washing machine all working at once might cause instantaneous black-out, and then where would you be? No. In Italy, it's best not to allude oneself with too many plans.

My friend Paolo is a *poi vediamo* Master. Otherwise, he's a pretty decent guy. Forcefully opinionated about useless theoretical issues, he is shamelessly non-committal when it comes to deciding anything practical. We argue often. Actually, I argue often. He usually just watches. Italians can never resist a good show. Once I am sufficiently worked up, he interrupts me and calmly states his case. "Uncertainty," he says, "is the only thing Italians can really count on. And that's not a bad thing. It adds thrill to life. It keeps us active and humble. Italy is the fifth richest nation in the world, but we could never be a superpower. Italians could never believe in actually having that much control over the state of the universe."

"But I don't want to know about the state of the universe," I protest, "I want to know if you're coming to the movies. For once, give me a straight answer. Why does it always have to be *poi vediamo?*"

"Because I don't know if the film will be possible."

"Paolo, the movie is starting in 35 minutes—and if we're going to go, *vediamo* NOW!"

As my impatience mounts, my friend tells me that part of the problem is grammatical. Italians use a present verb to express a future action. *Poi vediamo* is actually "later, we see." There's not a whole lot of room for planning in a language where tomorrow takes the present tense.

Despite my better judgment, I consider this linguistic possibility. As I do, I remember why we are friends. Paolo is bad at movie invitations and good at making up explanations. Unfortunately for me, I'm more entertained by explanations than I am by cinema.

When I tell him this, he is happy that I can recognize his virtues. "Of course," he smiles, "in Italy, you can easily find satisfaction in both. We are infamous for one and famous for the other."

Paolo never skips a beat. Maybe it is uncertainty that keeps the wit strong and the brain fit. It's a theory that has never been proven, of course, but someday we'll know the truth. *Poi vediamo.*

IDENTITY

Free Entrance

Entrata libera

There is no word for browsing in Italian.

T he shoppers who flock to Florence from all over the world come with the strange misconception that shopping in Italy is fun. Armani's class, Ferragamo's craftsmanship, a bit of Versace sparkle, and a dash of Valentino red might make you think so. Fun, however, is not exactly the word I would use. Intimidating is more like it. Baffling might work. Not that any of us usually admit it. Telling tourists that shopping in Italy is more excruciating than fun is like going to a Christmas party and telling your host's five-year-old that there is no Santa Claus. Besides, visiting shoppers are generally too anxious to fill their new Gucci luggage with San Lorenzo leather to be bothered with the likes of me and my Italian shopping traumas.

So, go ahead, immerse yourself body and soul in the joys of a city center shopping spree. It usually only takes about three *"entrata libera"* signs before you'll start wondering, "Free entrance? What exactly do they mean by that? After all, these are shops not museums. They certainly don't expect you to pay an entrance fee just for browsing, do they?"

Well, no. The *entrata libera* signs are there because there is actually no word for "browsing" in Italian. The concept of walking into a store without the slightest idea of what you will find in there or if you'll want to buy something once you do find out is a relatively new concept in Italy. Nonetheless, phantom shopping is not choice Italian entertainment. Let's just say that Italians don't find anything fun about picking through overstuffed clothes racks to find a bargain. Not that there are too many overstuffed racks or bargains in Italy in the first place. Mostly, when Italians walk into a shop they go with a purpose. Prior to stepping inside, Italians will deeply scrutinize the shop window and memorize everything the store has in stock. For most Italians this process takes about 3.5 seconds and is especially effective because most of the smaller shops display all of their merchandise in the window. Therefore, there's really no reason to browse. It's all right there for the whole strolling world to see.

"I want a pair of black trousers, size 42, wool-cotton mix, low waist, no pockets, narrow legs, crease in front, and hem turned up at the bottom, *per favore*," is what Italians say when they march into a store ready to make their purchase. Is there any room for browsing in all that?

Basically, in a society of secure shoppers and fashion experts, the *entrata libera* sign was designed to give customers permission to be indecisive. Does this mean that Italian shopkeepers expect you to buy just because you timidly venture over their threshold? In Florence, probably not. In an international city like this one, most clerks have probably had to get used to the idiosyncrasies of foreign shoppers who touch everything and buy nothing.

Francesca, a shop assistant in one of Florence's many specialty shops, explained, "At first it was shocking to see people wander into the shop and pull things off shelves without so much as a glance at me. It was like having someone come into my house and rummage through my drawers! But I have finally understood," continued Francesca with a smile, "that many foreign customers are used to looking with their hands. In Italy, we talk with our hands, but look with our eyes. It takes a little while to get used to, *ma va bene*, but it's okay, because it proves the world is a varied place."

So, happy shopping! But next time you are tempted to mosey *liberamente* into a central boutique, prepare yourself *psicologicamente* before entering. Then just march right in there with a click in your step and demand (yes, demand) to see the tailored cotton collar shirt with the pink and green butterfly motif you saw hanging in the window.

The clerk will ask your size, "*Che misura?*"

You will unflinchingly respond "*Una 44.*"

And you are sure to be friends.

To Do the Shopping

Fare lo shopping

When you do *"lo shopping"* in Italy,
forget about personal preference.

There are many advantages to shopping in Italy. Everyone knows that for high quality and chic designer clothes this is the place to buy. Besides, you will almost always come away with more than you bargained for, at least culturally speaking. One morning of healthy Italian shopping will teach you more about this country and its people than four years of Italian studies at a university. Discover how Italians shop and you will understand their priorities. And although shopping may not be a window to the Italian soul, it is certainly a window to their psyche.

But be advised, if you do decide to *fare lo shopping* in Italy, there are some things you should keep in mind. First, don't expect to find a shirt in your favorite color, or even in a color you need to match your beige slacks. It has been scientifically proven that in a given season all the shop windows boast the same shades, and if you are desperate for a pair of navy slacks when blue is not one of the two colors that stores have decided to stock that month, you are out of luck. Last season it was orange, turquoise, and avocado green. The fact that avocado green makes your skin look avocado green is of relevance to no one.

Second, when you do *lo shopping* in Italy, forget about personal preference. Although Italians may be secure shoppers with hawk eyes who immediately stake out the clothes they intend to buy, they are not known for being very adventurous in their purchases. Generally speaking, Italians won't dream of buying an outfit simply because they think it's cute. Around here, fashion is serious business, and people investing in an article of clothing solely on the grounds that they "like it" is improbable. Italians buy clothes to suit their bodies, and clothes to suit the times. That's all. Clothes should flatter the body, please the eye, and follow the fashion. Minor things like comfort or individual taste are secondary.

Lastly, before venturing down *via Tornabuoni*, reconcile yourself with the fact that *fare lo shopping* in Florence may force thee to know thyself and thy limitations. Perhaps one day Italy will be populated by salesclerks who work on commission and gush about how great you look in a gunny sack. As of now, Italians aren't so easily fooled. These days, a typical shop assistant has a haughty chin and high cheekbones. She will be aloof and smile sparingly. Young as she may seem, she is not a temp worker trying to save money for college. She has been there seven years. She will be there at least twenty more. That shop is her territory, her professional space, and those three dresses hanging on that rack are her field of expertise. Let her show you what she knows. After all, the woman knows her clothes. She also knows how her clothes look on your body. So until you learn to accurately judge clothes on the hanger before trying them on, you may be in for a little heartache.

Last January, during nationwide sales season, I tried on a green wool dress that I had unwittingly classified as "very cute." There I stood, turning indecisively in front of the fitting room mirror, until the saleslady interrupted my preening. "Take it off, you look like a nun." Amazing how easy it is to save seventy-five euro! Of course, she had every right to make the truth known to me. In a word-of-mouth society like Italy, there is no worse publicity than sending your customers around looking like convent escapees.

Fare lo shopping in Italy builds character. Whenever I feel myself on the verge of an existential crisis, I find it useful to subject myself to a Florentine shopping spree. Humbling and humiliating, it always puts me in my place. Fashion constraints and frank salesclerks serve to remind me of the insignificance of my desires. Try it. You'll come away with lovely clothes that suit you. They won't be the color you wanted or the cut you like, but then, in shopping as in life, compromise is key.

Another Year Older

Compiere gli anni

Most Italians have the habit of easing into their new year as if they were lowering themselves very slowly into an unheated pool.

If you want to have many birthdays, live in Italy. Together with Japan, Italy boasts the longest life span in the world. Thirty-six paid vacation days a year and the Mediterranean diet are probably partly responsible. Frequent art-filled walks and friendly piazza talks may also have something to do with it. Italy might not be the land of eternal youth, but it might just be the land of prolonged youth if you play your birthday cards right.

On the whole, Italians turn a year older without making too many waves. As far as I can see, there are several reasons for this. Firstly, most people have the habit of easing into their new year as if they were lowering themselves very slowly into a unheated pool. Aging is a one-step-at-a-time process designed to avoid the shock of a headfirst dive. Indeed, an Italian will almost always begin declaring their new age months before they actually have their birthday. In fact, when an Italian asks you how old you are, what they really want to know is the age you will be by the end of the year. In this country, if you turn thirty on the second of November, you will have probably said goodbye to your twenties as early as April.

Another reason that Italians take birthdays in stride lies in the virtue of their language. My friend Donatella explained it to me one day. "In English, you are forced to speak about age using the unfortunate question, 'How old are you?' It's not at all reasonable that even a child born last year be tagged old. With all the politically correct language zealots in your country, you'd think someone would have modified that phrase. Being old so early is detrimental to the psyche. The Italian form of the question," my friend continued, "has none of the same ominous implications. *Quanti anni hai*, how many years do you have? Makes years sound like prized possessions that have to be earned." To Donatella, there was a pleasantness in the question, as if someone were asking how many baseball cards you've collected or how many glass marbles you've stowed in your treasure jar. The more years you have, of course, the wealthier you are.

Even the Italian answer to the *anni* question is much more sophisticated than its English-language equivalent. "*Quanti anni hai?*" you may ask. "I'm in the class of '72," will be the veiled reply. In Italy, this is how most people will get around saying their age. Unfortunately, you are expected to do your own math, and if you're like me, you'll seldom bother. I'd rather it remain a mystery than actually have to do subtraction in my head. But if you are a natural mathematician and have no aversion to simple arithmetic, it may help you to know that "class of '72" does not stand for the year that person graduated from school. Their "class" refers to the year of their birth.

But there is one more reason why years in Italy fly by with grace and ease. And that is, when it's your birthday, you're expected to give rather than get. As Italians see it, you are the one who should be the happiest about your own birth. Therefore, it's logical that you be held responsible for most of the celebrating. In Italy, there's no sense of self-importance attached to blatantly making a big to-do about your own birthday. You are allowed, even expected, to bounce down the hall greeting every colleague you meet by saying, "*Oggi compio gli anni*, today I fulfil my years." Certainly, the use of "fulfil" here implies some sense of duty or obligation. It's up to you to make the world a happier place, at least on that one day a year that belongs to you.

So bring in cream puffs for your colleagues. Take your friends for *prosecco* in the piazza. And if you go out to eat, be the one to treat and not the one to be treated. Fulfil your years the Italian way, because it is said that to be giving is the best way to stay forever young.

Familiarity

La familiarità

It is lonely to see a face one time only.

If you want to be successful in Italy, get yourself a news agent. Mine is called Matteo. He sells papers, but his news is free because he sees it as his duty to tell you everything you need to know. Should you try the new *trattoria* at *Porta Romana*? Should you run back upstairs and get your umbrella? Is it best to wait until Thursday to exchange your dollars? He'll tell you if the trains are running, if via Cavour has been closed off, or if you should hurry to the corner shop for sheets on sale at a good price.

I pass his stand daily to collect my newspaper and he takes my spare change and questions with the grace worthy of his nickname, *l'ambasciatore di Firenze*, the Ambassador of Florence. For many of us who don't know any better, Matteo is an island of customer service in an ocean of indifferent bank clerks and stale bureaucrats. "It's difficult to get good customer service in Italy," I told him one morning.

"Not at all," was his reply. "Italians are easily capable of bending over backwards to help a client. We also quickly bend rules, reach creative compromises, and grant sizable favors. But there is no investment to be made in the casual customer. It is lonely to see a face one time only. *Noi contiamo sulla familiarità*. We count on familiarity."

A-ha! Loads has been said about the importance of family in Italy. But if family is first in this culture, then familiarity comes in second. Expectations are the motor of a society. Know a country's social expectations and you will understand that country. Italians do not expect to be treated well if they are wearing the face of a stranger. *La familiarità* means power in Italy. If you are familiar, then you have clout. If you walk through a door daily, you can expect a smile, a discount, or a piece of priceless advice. If you are just moseying through for your rightful slice of customer service, you'll often find your plate empty in Italy. In a word, *la familiarità* is the prerequisite for customer service.

"When a customer comes by, I like to be reminded that there is a world out there. Tell me a joke or what the politicians are doing to ruin our country, and if you can do both at the same time, it's even better," Giovanni, the fruit vendor at the *Sant'Ambrogio* market, told me recently. Does he save the best grapes for the customer with the best joke? "Of course!" he exclaimed. "And none of that sterile garbage without seeds. My grapes are virile!"

In Italy, if you want real grapes, real attention, and even real affection, become a familiar face. The most common word for "favor" in Italian is *piacere*, which doubles as a word for pleasure. "It is my pleasure to do you a pleasure. If you are familiar, then I'll see you around, and my kindness and compromise will be returned to me," is the common attitude. After all, the city is small and statistics show you are not going anywhere. Here, people prefer working in their own cities rather than filling their pockets with another town's money. University students seldom go away to college. Children play *bandiera genovese*, "capture the flag," in the same courtyards where their parents played. In Italian, there is no word for hometown. If it is your town, it is obvious that it's also your home. Anything else would be adulterous.

So customer familiarity is widely expected and easily achieved. If no one knows you, they will most certainly know your family. Or at the very least, they will know whose family your house belonged to in the fifteenth century. Those rich bankers, merchants, artists, or architects, as the case may be, are what made the town what it is today. Roots are respected. They can be your roots or someone else's, but as long as you establish a connection, any connection, it will somehow ground you. "Know that your existence comes from somewhere, and make those roots known to me." That is the essence of *la familiarità*. It may seem like a lot to ask of the woman who comes in to buy a piece of bread at the *forno*, but it will pay off for her, too. If she comes often enough, they will set her square of *schiacciata* aside so that it's ready in the morning when she stops by at her usual hour.

'In House'

In casa

"Don't worry, Honey. They say the thousandth meeting feels a lot like the first."

All I could hope for was that he would leave
before my relatives started commenting on
the way his ears stuck out.

Just before Christmas last year, my cousin Marianna announced that she would be inviting her boyfriend, Tierri, *in casa*. She had been going out with him for a year and a half. They had been going to school together since middle school. He had been over innumerable times as a member of Marianna's *compagnia*, or group of regular friends. But this would be the first time Tierri would cross the threshold as Marianna's formal suitor. We were all supposed to be on our best behavior.

In order to understand the big formal deal of officially introducing a boyfriend *in casa*, one must start considering that Italy is essentially an outdoor society. There's no room inside people's homes for it to be otherwise. Perhaps that's why it usually takes a few years for Italian parents to let their children's boyfriends or girlfriends into the house. Young people usually have to walk about the piazza together for several months at least before they are "allowed" indoors. But they actually prefer it that way because, in this country, there is more privacy to be found on the street than in the home. Before the *in casa* introduction, if the young couple does come into the house, they are usually accompanied by at least eight other friends. Such *compagnia* is often the best way to ensure that involved parties remain anonymous and uninvolved. In Italy, times are changing, but traditionally, introductions that imply some sort of personal, emotional commitment have always been considered quite an ordeal and are put off for as long as possible.

So it was Christmas and my cousin's boyfriend was finally

coming to court the family. I had been in Italy long enough to know that poor Tierri would already have several strikes against him before he even entered *in casa*. First of all, his name. What nationality was it? Certainly not Italian. What apostle was responsible for it? His name itself offered no guarantees. Second, Tierri's father was rumored to root for the soccer team from Torino. Like father, like son, they say, and what were we going to do with a *Juventus* fan at our table? Third, my grandmother had seen his mother at Gianni Ciccio's, and she was apparently known for buying bruised fruit. What kind of woman would feed her men ugly fruit? These would be the main issues weighing on my family's mind.

What I couldn't understand, though, was that if Tierri was finally to be formally introduced *in casa*, couldn't my cousin have chosen a more discreet holiday? Was it really necessary for this poor soul to be subjected to all of us at once and on such a momentous occasion? *Mamma mia!* All I could hope for was that he would leave before my relatives started commenting on the way his ears stuck out. Then again, maybe having Tierri *in casa* at Christmas was a good strategy. A ploy to tap into the Christmas spirit. Everyone would be full, benevolent, and preoccupied with winning at Bingo. I just hoped Tierri had sense enough not to win.

Despite my worries, the holiday *in casa* went well. The *tortelli* were tender and swollen with tasty broth. The boiled cow tongue suited everyone's holiday taste buds. The tree's flickering candles were beautiful, and no one but me was worried about the blatant fire hazard. The men happily offered their *vin santo*, and the women proudly brought forth their anise and almond *biscotti*. All the children were invited to stand on their chairs and recite Christmas poems.

Applause was frequent. My uncle was allowed to turn on his Austrian yodeling carols and his sons swallowed their complaints. It was Christmas. The tablecloth was dusty with powdered sugar and all was right in the world.

Finally, at around ten, Tierri got up to leave the table. He had stayed for an appropriate amount of time. Now he and Marianna could leave, go out for some fresh air, and meet friends who had had to stand before similar juries.

As soon as their seats were safely empty, the table became full of animated conversation. My family sat exchanging dried figs and fresh opinions. *He's as good as bread, poor guy. Let's hope he has a lot of bread, if he wants to keep Miss Marianna Monroe happy. Let's hope he's rich and stupid. Rich is nothing if she cannot persuade him. But did you see his ears? Their first child will be called Dumbo.*

"Oh well," I thought. "Welcome to the family, Tierri. You've passed the test. They're talking grandchildren."

A Dying Race

Una razza morente

They blame money and late marriages,
but if no one's having babies now, it's
still *il Duce*'s fault.

When my upstairs neighbor finds an article she thinks I can't live without reading, she tapes it to a packaged *merendina* snack and throws it at my head as I pass under her window. Not a photocopy, the original. *Signora* Norma never worries about keeping information for herself.

The first article that hit me claimed that there are two types of women in the world. Some women have "apple-shaped" bodies, others have "pear-shaped" ones. "See," she told me afterward, "I am an Apple, and you are a Pear." That was before Italy had taught me not to be too hypersensitive when people compare you to a fruit. Since then though, I've never been able think of another way to describe my neighbor. She had slim legs, and a strong, full upper body. Everything about Norma is wide, round, and firm. Even her gray hair must have been red once.

"*L'Italia è una razza morente*, Italy is a dying race," Norma called to me the other morning as she leaned out to drop me her newest find. "They blame money and late marriages, but if no one's having babies now, it's still *il Duce*'s fault."

Normally, I would love to stop and chat with elderly ladies about Mussolini's guilty conscience, but that day I was late even by Italian standards. "I'll read the article," I called, "*Ma ora devo proprio scappare*! Now I have to run!*"

Italian journalists write about demographics a lot these days. Maybe because Italy boasts the lowest birthrate in the world and it makes sense to no one. We are, after all, talking about a traditionally Catholic and infamously family-oriented society. Nonetheless, the eighties saw the Italian birthrate slide below zero. Although the figure has fought its way upward of late, most affirm that the increase is primarily due to births in immigrant families rather than Italian ones.

According to Norma's article, Italy's low birthrate is the result of urbanization in the 1950s. It was then that children stopped being a resource and started being an expense. In the cramped quarters of city living, *bambini* started to mean more mouths to feed and less air to breathe. These days, most couples blame "lack of money" as the primary cause for "lack of children." The article made no mention at all of Mussolini and left me wondering what Norma had meant.

Certainly, *il Duce* has been blamed for many things. But now it seemed that his ghost was somehow guilty too. I knocked on her door that afternoon, intent on getting her point straight. Once comfortably settled in her best chair, I had to drink a *Crodino* and eat three pieces of her Spanish marzipan before she would explain.

Mussolini related childbirth with military power and fertility with national virility. According to his program, Italy's position in the world depended, first and foremost, on the amount of patriots its women bore and raised. During the Fascist regime, motherhood was the most complete form of female patriotism. "Mussolini gave women worth through childbirth," Norma explained. "Pregnant ladies would parade in front of his balcony and yell, '*E*' *tuo, Duce*, this child is yours.' Mussolini needed children to fight his wars. He gave gold medals to women with many children. Mothers grew the babies in their bellies, but once delivered, they belonged to the state." Norma shook her head. "*Eh, sì, 'madre' vuol dire 'martire.'* It was true in those days. 'Mother' meant 'martyr.'"

"My mother got her medal too—because there were eight of us. And *il Duce* sent us strong, black cloth so she could make us school smocks." She smiled sadly from the memory. *"Poi ci ha mandato buoni per comprare fagioli, farina, e zoccoli da indossare.* And he sent us coupons to buy beans, cornmeal, and clogs to wear. None of us in the country had shoes then. With clogs, my people felt like gentlemen. He tricked us that way. Nothing to eat, but something to cover our feet with, you know?"

No, Norma. There is so much I don't know. Still, she was willing to share a piece of history with me and, most importantly, find the knot that tied it to today. With the Fascists, women had babies as a political favor to their leader. With the Party's fall, people stopped having children, *per dispetto*, out of spite. If many babies had been a sign of patriotism, then few babies quickly became a sign of protest. "Do you see?" Norma asked anxiously. "First seven children, now just one in an effort to undo *il Duce*. He is why we are *una razza morente.*" She grinned, happy to have solved the mystery for me.

I smiled back at her. My elderly apple-shaped neighbor was beautiful, and I couldn't wait to read the next piece of news that would fly from her open window.

Recommended

Raccomandato

Italy is a tribal society. It feeds on two main resources: blood and favors.

Some say that to get a good cup of coffee in Italy you need to be friends with the barman. It is also said that to get hired in this country you have to be friends with the boss. Well, maybe you don't have to be friends exactly, as in chums who barbecue fat Florentine steaks together at his house in Chianti on weekends, but you do need to be friendly with him in some way. A friend of a friend of a friend or the son or nephew of a friend of a friend will suffice.

"If you get hired in Italy, it's almost impossible to be fired," explains Enrico, my newly graduated architect friend. He has been working for free in a studio for six months and considers the position a favor from his uncle. "In this country, hiring someone is like playing the stock market. It's a risk and a gamble. You let someone onto your payroll and they will be there for life. So it's best to choose someone *raccomandato*."

To be *raccomandato* or "recommended," means more than one might assume at first glance. We are not talking about a simple letter of recommendation signed by a previous employer that vouches for your professional expertise. In Italy, to be "recommended" means that the job is virtually yours, as in favor rendered, favor due.

There are, of course, exceptions, Enrico admits. In some cases, resumes will be looked at, tests taken, and interviews held. Sometimes the best candidate wins. But it doesn't hurt if the best candidate also knows someone. Certainly, favoritism can happen just about anywhere. In Italy, though, it's not just that it can happen, it is the way the game is actually played.

"Fundamentally," Enrico tells me, "Italy is a tribal society.

It feeds on two main resources: blood and favors. They are the oil that keeps the economy's wheels turning."

Enrico's comment may sound strange, but it's not hard to see. In sectors as diverse as food, fashion, and engineering, Italian big business has traditionally been family-run. Ferrari, Ferragamo, Fiat, and Versace are just a few examples of how business in Italy builds bridges with blood ties. Sons and daughters and, at worst, nieces and nephews, often fill high administrative and executive positions in the companies created by their biological founding fathers. According to tribal logic, it's about keeping the money and creativity safely flowing within the family.

On a smaller scale, it's also worthwhile to mention that Italy's network of local family-run businesses still occupies a considerable portion of the market, particularly for products of high craftsmanship. Small businesses are often notorious in their efforts to avoid the risk of investing in a well-qualified "stranger." In most cases, small companies will unanimously choose an almost-qualified familiar face as a better bet on which to place their money.

Favors are the other lubricant keeping the Italian economy healthy, or at least well-oiled. In this country, it's a widespread conviction that any state-run establishment, any system, any government will only bleed us for taxes and complicate our plans. In this "us against them" set-up, it's the individual's job to form enough solid favor-exchanging relationships to make the list of "us" stronger and longer than the list of "them." The family is the central dot, but the circle is meant to expand, like a drop of ink on Japanese silk paper.

So hurry, get into someone's circle and make it a pleasure to owe you a favor. It will come back to you in no time at all.

And we'll assume that you have time. Regional statistics say that you will be going nowhere. If you are in Italy now, just wait and see. This city will get into your blood and to leave it will be like leaving your dearly beloved to step into another's life.

Togetherness

Tutti insieme appassionatamente

In this family, one more plate means nothing.

66 When you have writer's block, go talk to a five-year -old. It will give you something to say again." That's what my creative writing professor in college used to say. My trip to Murano last weekend proved a chance to take her advice.

I am lucky to belong to one of the last big families in northern Italy. Modern Italy is a myriad of only-child households, but my aunt and uncle are the exception to the rule. If you need a kid between the ages of four and seventeen to talk to, their house is the place to go. I crossed the island in ten minutes and, as is usual in Murano, ran into my cousin Elisabetta before I made it to her house.

"I was just coming to see you," I told her.

"Good," she said, kissing both my cheeks. "Are you staying for dinner?"

I like my cousin. Elisabetta will be eighteen in June. She is the oldest of nine children, and the only girl. I told her I'd like to stay over. There is no need to wait for her parents' permission. In this family, one more plate means nothing.

The two of us ran her errands together and made it home just before the *risotto* turned to glue. At the table, I was happily squeezed between a pirate and a fireman. Both were allowed to keep their hats on during dinner, as long as they kept their elbows off the table. Needless to say, my aunt and uncle choose their battles. Two of the other boys were not so lucky and got kitchen door patrol. No roller skates or hammers in the eating room. When each boy finally found his place, their father raised his glass and thanked God that we were together and had food to eat. He asked that we may someday learn to be kind in this world. On that cue, Stefano stopped kicking my legs. The long tablecloth hid everything.

That night's dinner topics were big ears and how easy it is to come home wearing someone else's coat. I nudged my five-year-old cousin Davide as he was finishing his *risotto*, "I need to write a story about Italy. What do you think I should write about?"

He didn't need to think about his answer. He wanted me to write about his world. *"Scrivi sulle famiglie numerose,* write about families with many children. And about the gigantic chocolate egg we get at Easter."

Okay. It was months until Easter and almost no one in Italy has a big family anymore, but Davide was right. The size of that *fondente* egg was worth mentioning, and a story about prolific families wasn't too much to ask for after so much talk about low birthrate. As far as Davide was concerned, the race is certainly not dying, and it seems right to give his view a voice, too.

After dinner, Wendy and her Lost Boys settled on watching *The Sound of Music,* which in Italian is called *Tutti insieme, appassionatamente,* or All Together, Passionately. My cousins knew the words by heart and each person got a character. Elisabetta, of course, is forced to be Julie Andrews. The most successful scene performed by my cousins was the one in the convent when the nuns sing "How do you solve a problem like Maria?" Ten years ago, Elisabetta decided to change the words to "How do you solve a problem like Mattia?" in honor of her oldest younger brother. The next year, after Mattia had done his time, the song became "How do you solve a problem like Pietro?" And so on down the line. This year it was Davide's turn. The three youngest boys put blankets on their heads and made very pious nuns of themselves.

We made it to the scene when Frauline Maria decides to make the curtains into clothes for the kids, and the TV splutters out. My cousins took turns pounding with no luck at all. It seemed there was nothing left to do but become a version of the Von Trapp family ourselves. Pietro went for his guitar and led us in mountain folk songs. Luckily, we avoided anything as tame as Edelweiss. Our songs recalled the good old days when mountain peaks were made of *polenta* and rivers flowed with *ragù*. There was also a verse about whipped dried codfish. We sang in Venetian, Italian, and English. "The Saints Go Marching In" meant bedtime for the younger half of the brood. My cousins are named for the apostles, and I find the song quite apropos.

With only five kids left in the living room, my aunt and uncle stretched out and enjoyed the quiet. "You know, *Amore*," my uncle grinned mischievously at his wife, "that curtain thing might not be such a bad idea."

Elisabetta shook her finger at her father. "*Neanche per sogno Papà*, don't even dream about it." She's told me before that although being part of a *famiglia numerosa* has its challenges, she wouldn't trade her Lost Boys in for anything in the world. Tonight she turned to me and rolled her eyes, "You have to draw the line at drapes, you know?"

"*Sì*, I suppose you're right," her father agreed.

In the Italian scale of values, fashion doesn't come before family, but it's best not to push things too far.

The Azzurri

Gli Azzurri

Last time we waved that flag,
they had a picnic on our heads.

When *gli Azzurri*, the Italian National Football team, is together on the field, Italy's citizens lose their local fervor and just call themselves Italian. Other times they are *Veneziani, Fiorentini, Romani,* or *Siciliani.* Other times they walk their regional walk and talk their regional talk. When those blue-shirted fellows, *gli Azzurri,* step into the stadium, regional pride dies, or at least goes dormant, for two forty-five-minute time slots and one long commercial break.

"*Siamo tutti italiani quando giochiamo a calcio,* we are all Italian when we play soccer," my student Paolo Galletti told me last Friday. "It is Italy's only form of patriotism." Paolo is a banker from Arezzo who makes the forty-five minute drive to Florence only when he absolutely must. Arezzo and Florence were enemies in the fourteenth century, you see, and the antagonism still runs strong in his blood today. Now that I had him in Florence I was going to bleed him dry. Paolo is one of my favorite students. He pays me to teach him Business English, and, among faxes and business correspondence, he gives me weekly Italian cultural analysis for free.

"Patriotism in Italy is nothing like the flag-waving, parade-going, band-playing, summer picnic atmosphere you find on Independence Day in the United States," he told me wryly. "Last time we waved that flag, they had a picnic on our heads."

I nodded. In Italy most families still have members who remember the Fascist years. Memories of Mussolini's search for *l'Italianità* still foster feelings that patriotism is a vice rather than a virtue. *Il Duce*'s patriotic dream sought after the splendor of ancient Rome and was founded on "moral" bellicose activity, totalitarian government, and autocracy. Let's just say that Italy's brief affair with patriotism ended badly. Italians don't like to think they will let themselves fall for it again. Paolo continued, "We found out the hard way that patriotism means that you're either extraordinarily simplistic or quite fanatic. *Entrambi non convengono ad un italiano,* neither is a convenient thing for an Italian. It has proved best to keep our passion for the playing field. Italians can afford to be patriotic at the stadium, but only there."

Soccer is safe, really. The field is clearly delineated, fouls are called immediately, and the results are evident after ninety minutes. Ninety minutes of proud Italian identity. In truth, it was not the cultural movements of the nineteenth century intellectual elite nor the battles fought in two world wars that succeeded in creating an Italian identity. The efforts of modern political systems and Italy's constant race to establish itself as a world power have failed to achieve widespread patriotic sentiment. That's why Paolo will smilingly tell you, "Soccer has succeeded where everything else has failed."

Stadium patriotism works out quite well. *Gli Azzurri* play for everyone and are careful never to step on anyone's regional toes. At the end of the match the *Fiorentini, Veneziani, Milanesi,* and *Siciliani* are allowed to put on their regional clothes. They return to their own piazzas, pick up their precious vernacular, wallow in regional humor, and affirm their own superiority, because no one in Italy makes steak or squid or pesto sauce just so. Once *gli Azzurri* retire for the night, each city's citizens remember what they own. The Renaissance belongs to Florence, and Venice has dibs on the doorway to the Orient. Rome still rules all of the Western world. The Neapolitan and his humor is still king-jester of the Kingdom of Naples, and the Sicilian still looks at the Italian mainland as part of the European continent rather than part of his own pride and joy, at least until the next time *La Nazionale* plays and Italy becomes unified once more. The welcomed "Blues" carry our improvised national pride onto the field, kicking our position on the globe around like a soccer ball. The flag is hung from window sills and, for an hour and a half, people are allowed to forget that it was Mussolini's tri-colored excuse for two decades of power and struggle.

As we ended last week's lesson, Paolo summed it up for me. "In essence, Italy's flag should not be red, white, and green. People from all regions have to admit that. We may agree on nothing else, but everyone knows *che l'Italia ha un cuore azzurro*, Italy has a heart that's blue."

I smile. It's good when students teach teachers. It makes one think that all is right in the world.

The *Qua o Là* Question

Here or there?

It's like comparing cherries and watermelon.

Anyone who has spent more than three months living in Italy knows the *Qua o Là* question well. If you're an expatriot and a bohemian you've surely mulled it over in outdoor cafes. If you've spent a third of your life in this country, you've probably stopped answering. That's fine. You can try to ignore it, but trust me, it will follow you anyway.

"Ti piace di più qua o là?" Everyone wants to know, "Do you like it better here or there?" I've been asked this question at least three times at every dinner party I've gone to for the past thirteen years, so you'd think that by now I'd have found my answer. Alas, I haven't. Personally, my "here" happens to be Italy and my "there" is California, or vice versa, but no matter the country I find myself dining in, the dinner party crowd is always very curious to know which one I "like better." *"Non si possono confrontare,* one can't compare," I always say. By being diplomatic people think I'm trying to avoid hurting their feelings when, in reality, it's not their feelings I'm worried about. It's my own peace of mind. Although it's easy to love two places, it's not always easy to compare them. There are certain health risks that come with trying to constantly have such heavy things on your mind. Comparing Italy and the United States is not like comparing apples and oranges, it's like comparing cherries and watermelon.

But sometimes I get careless and dive headfirst into the futile search for the answer to *qua o là*. I start by telling myself wonderful stories about Italy in a land-of-Oz way and somehow always end up thinking about how rare it is to be alone in an Italian house. There are never enough rooms. And there are not enough elevators and there are too many stairs. And the people going up always have something to say to the people going down. All the doors creak loudly; it's too easy to know when they're being opened, and it's very hard to keep them shut. Then I muse over the fact that no one in Italy ever sits on the floor or walks barefoot. They sometimes eat fruit with a fork. They litter and tell you their trash is biodegradable. They cut in line and eat raw artichokes with olive oil that looks like liquid gold. They let their children pour a spot of coffee into their milk and a spot of wine into their water, and there is nothing immoral about it. There are crosses hung on the walls in banks and it's not a matter of religion or politics. It's just a part of history. The floors are marble and cold, and the terraces smell of clean clothes and sunlight.

Right around the time I find myself musing over laundry, I switch gears and start thinking about the United States. It is very easy to be alone in an American house. There are built-in locks on every door, and no one sees their neighbors regularly. Most public doors open themselves. Litterbugs are seen as dredges of society. In the United States, schools are made with quasi-cardboard walls and carpets are installed in every bank. There are loony tunes and show tunes and movie theaters open even in August with lines of people weaving around the building. People are crazy about roller coasters, play board games at dinner parties, and often quote Benjamin Franklin and Bob Hope. Hands-on discovery museums and tailgate picnics are well loved. Ladies wear flat shoes. Kids learn to square dance at school and they make state maps with detergent and starch for educational purposes. American adults can play in toy stores, read poetry in college cafes, and spend all day getting watery coffee stains on new books in bookstores.

There. The essence of cultural identity in two sacks on each plate of the scale. And yes, these definitions are painfully inadequate. Well, so am I. And so are my countries. But they are also unique, diverse, and very close to my heart.

The bottom line is that living well in a country means learning to enjoy the gifts it has to offer. Loving its language is like eating its ripest summer fruit. It could just be me, but Italian words are like cherries and feel the same way in your mouth. Communication in English is more like eating a very good watermelon. It is possible to love both flavors with equal intensity. It's about savoring the sweetness, and remembering to safely spit out the pits.

Qua o là?

Neither. Both here and there.

Acknowledge-

M̲y first *grazie* goes to my parents, Robert and Lucia Falcone, for their constant, unfailing support. To my family, Nicole and Sebastiano Padoan, Chiara Falcone, and Joyce and Bill Anderson, my first and kindest critics. Thank you to the Barbini and Fuga families for making this country so precious a place. Special thanks to Margherita Barbini and Giuseppe Biscontin and Carlotta and Leonardo Biscontin for the role they played in making Italy home to me.

There are many who made this book possible. Heartfelt thanks to Tony and Nita Tucker for believing the idea could become a book. Many thanks to Marco Badiani for the efforts it took to make it really happen, and to *The Florentine* crew Giovanni Giusti and Antonio Lo Iacono. Special thanks to Leo Cardini for his wonderful drawings and tireless enthusiasm.

Lastly, thank you to all those unmentioned here, who somehow appear within the pages of this book. Inspiration is an easy thing when your characters already exsist.

Grazie mille.

Linda Falcone

Born in Northern California and raised in a bilingual family with an Italian mother and American father, Linda Falcone has been traveling between her two countries of origin since birth.

After completing her studies in English and Italian at the University of California, Davis and l'Università di Venezia, she decided to never give up the joys of culture shock.

Celebrating her fourteenth year of permanent Italian living, Linda now lives and teaches in Florence, Italy.

Leo Cardini

Florentine by birth and artist by nature, Leo Cardini never leaves anything undrawn. Graduate of l'Istituto d'Arte in Florence, he has experimented with every form of visual art.

Creator of hundreds of comics and logos, painter of acrylics and murals, Leo is also a wine connoisseur, world traveler, fanatic Fiorentina fan, photographer and father.

He has been a partner in Agile Logica graphic design studio since 2000, and his art, like good Tuscan wine, improves with age.